Crackin' Up!

28 Days of Letting in the Light

Lisa M. Smith, M.S., Msc.D., Ph.D.

Blessed are the cracked.
For they shall let in the light.

~ Diane English ~

To you. To me. For we are one in the same.

… to my Goddess Friends…
you <u>know</u> who you are!
Thank you for reminding me of my light,
or shining yours upon me when
mine had grown dim.

…make me an instrument of Thy Peace!

Dear New Friend,

I was tucking my daughter in when she was three-years-old one night and like most three-year-olds, she was feeling scared of the dark. In addition to the nightlight, she asked me to leave the door open. She said, "Just a crack for an itty bit of light, Mommy – that's all I need." I recognized how true it is that just a "crack" of light can illuminate a great deal of darkness and oh, how safe that little bit of light can make us feel!

There are many definitions for crack. In general, it means that a space has opened up – that something (the old) is breaking apart. It is making way for something new. I think of a bird egg that is cracking open – it is making way for the baby bird to come out. If the egg never cracked, the bird could never be free.

Over the course of my life, I've been cracked a time or two. Although I didn't appreciate the opening-up at the time, what seeped in changed me and I am who I am today because of it all. Currently, as a single mother of 5 (4 of my children now grown), I have learned a lot about letting in light. When my son was diagnosed with autism, I was cracked. When I divorced (for the second time), I was cracked. When I ended an emotionally abusive relationship, I was cracked. When I moved over 15 times in twenty years (no, I was NOT in the witness protection program! ☺), I was cracked. When I filed for bankruptcy, lost my house, returned to the workforce after being home with my children for 17 years, I was cracked. As I spent years as a single mom, working many jobs **and** going to school I found lots of cracks in the form of *great big* fears!

Life cracks us – it's supposed to – when all you "thought you were" lies scattered all over the floor – it can look and feel pretty messy. But in this space, there are endless possibilities available and from this raw material, we get to create something new. So, I invite you to join me – in this moment, one crack at a time – to let in the light.

Crackin' up – that's what this book is about. Opening up a crack to let in an "itty bit of light" into the darkened places of our minds, bodies, and spirits. Cracking open some space to make room for something new to come forth.

I'm crackin' up – care to join me? Oh, and by the way – I found another meaning of the phrase "crackin' up" along the way - a sense of humor. Yeah…I began to allow life to just crack me open and then crack me up. Not taking everything so seriously has allowed me to put some space around all the things that were happening. In so doing, I found plenty of room to play and let in the light!

Happy Crackin'!
Lisa

Welcome frustration.
It is a gift that says we need to
change something.
~ Unknown ~

It is possible to move a mountain
by carrying away small stones.
~ Chinese proverb ~

Introduction

When my son was younger, he loved cars and one day, he was crying because he had lost his "no one" car. We searched everywhere for this mysterious car. I had no idea what he was talking about! Finally, a few days later, he came in elated, holding the cherished "no one" car. I looked at the side of it and it had "No. 1" printed on the side. I laughed and got it! My literal son!

But, it is analogous to how we all feel sometimes – like we are "no one" when in fact, we truly are No. 1! We just get lost in our erroneous beliefs (most of which were handed to us by someone else), patterns, habits, and relationships that support the "no one" idea instead of the No. 1 Truth!

This book is about changing the way we look at ourselves & treat ourselves– one day at a time. It is divided into 28 days. This seemed the right amount of time – especially as women, we have a cycle that typically lasts 28 days and it easily breaks down into 4 segments of 7 (7 days in a week). So, each day of the week, we focus on something different.

For the next 28 days, you and I are going to go on a journey. Kinda like an adventurous girlfriend road trip. I love a good road trip – don't you? We're going to set our GPS (Goddess Positioning System!) to *Lighten*

Up, HERE & NOW and see where it takes us! And…what's a good road trip without music? I have selected a theme song or two for each of the 4 segments – one for each day of the week. Feel free to fill in your own, if you'd rather! Make a playlist and hum right along with me!

Here's an overview of the weeks:

Manifest It! Mondays
Free – Joss Stone
Break My Stride – Matthew Wilder

What do you want out of our life? Do you see yourself as the driver of your car (i.e. life) or are you a passenger? Do you have a clear vision of the road ahead, or is it one big blur? Is there a *Dead End* sign ahead or do you have many paths to choose on your journey? Here we shine the light on ourselves and our intentions. We are going to talk to ourselves and find out what we want (and do not want). *You* get to decide how much light and into which crack(s) you shall be shining it into…one small step at a time.

Treat Me Right Tuesdays
Free Your Mind – En Vogue
Eye of the Tiger - Survivor

Tuesdays are dedicated to our health. We explore how we are treating this car (yes, we're going to beat this analogy to death! ☺) we are driving. Are you in a beautiful, souped up sports car with trick rims or are you falling apart on the side of the road in need of a serious tow?! In our car analogy, if your tires are flat and your engine is not working, simply changing your oil, or fuel choice isn't the answer – we're talking about a tune-up. From the inside-out. But, we'll look at some easy ways to integrate healthy things into your life. Remember small cracks. Lettin' in the light…one small step at a time!

How I Wonder & Wander Wednesdays
Wide-Open Spaces – Dixie Chicks
Defying Gravity - Wicked

Wednesday we're going to wonder and wander around in the wide-open spaces of why we do what we do. We'll look at our beliefs. We'll wonder…how we resist what shows up in our lives, how we view what shows up in our lives, how we fear what shows up in our lives (or what *will* show up) and how we accept (or don't) what shows up in our lives. We'll wander in to some dark spaces and wonder how to create a little more space…one small step at a time!

We're In This Thing Together Thursdays
We Are Family – Sister Sledge
Seasons of Love – Rent Soundtrack

Thursdays are dedicated to looking at how we relate to our world, our significant relationships - with ourselves, with others and relationships with our (or other) children. We also illuminate things (or people) we need to let go of. We're shining a light on our own being, and how that is reflected back to us through our relationships. We're looking for harmony that resonates from within…one small step at a time.

Fun, Fun & More Fun Fridays!
Make Your Own Kind of Music – Mama Cass Elliot
Pocketful of Sunshine – Natasha Bedingfield

This day is about creating and playing – from journaling, painting, dancing, and singing to anything your play-filled wanderlust-self can dream-up to do! This is about re-connecting to that adventurous little girl-Goddess-Princess - who could do and BE **anything!** We're going to join her in her space of play and possibilities and find a way to bring that into our lives here and now. We do not stop playing because we grow old. We grow old because we stop playing. That's gonna stop 'a right now…one small step at a time!

Me & My Shadow Saturday
Uncharted – Sara Bareilles
Brave – Sara Bareilles

On these days we will explore a little bit of our patterns and beliefs that hold us hostage. We'll peer into our "shadow self." We'll look at beliefs that might be keeping us from seeing what really *is* and what really wants to happen. This is not a huge excavation into our childhoods. Sometimes that is necessary and if you have not done that, I recommend you do that with a skilled therapist. This is about looking into our pasts for clues as to what we're holding onto here and now that might be holding us captive. It's time to expose the shadow a bit and all we need is just an "itty bit" of light…one small step at a time.

Sacred Serenity Sundays
Rejoice – Il Divo
Thankful – Josh Grobin

These days we will be finding and exploring a connection to something greater than ourselves. Some call this God, others call it Universe, Spirit, Great Spirit, Divine Energy, Source...many names for one concept. It is the sacred energy that breathes us, grows our fingernails and co-creates with us. Whatever you call your Source, we'll be exploring our *essence* and our connection to that energy that is in and all around us. If we were to use our car analogy (and you *knew* I would!), our car would represent our bodies, but we are NOT our cars. It's just a vehicle (pun intended) to use while we are here learning what we do. On these days, we'll look at what's going on inside the car...one small step at a time.

~

I'm sure you haven't missed my oh, so subtle endings, "one small step at a time." This is not about another diet, makeover, or punishing ourselves in any way, shape or form! We want to infuse our mind, bodies and spirits with so much light & love that it just squeezes out anything that no longer serves our highest and best selves! We're so worth it! This is about being kind, gentle, non-judgmental but *mostly* loving to make incremental changes *one small step at a time.* Which, if you think about it is the only thing you *can* do...otherwise, we call that falling!

You can approach this book from many different angles. I'm all about choices. My hope is that you feel into that which works best for YOU! You can focus on one concept and really integrate that one concept over the month or you can focus on all aspects of yourself, implementing slight movements in each area and repeat each month for the next year. I am setting the intention that you will find the exact perfect balance for you.

Also, at the end of each day there are several "fill in" spots (for a gratitude – a good and not so good – where we get to crack open a belief about the 'not so good' – can we find the blessing? Crack.) We'll also create a declaration (I've provided one to jump-start your "I Do Declare" muscle!). I also explain my not-so-conventional view of an affirmation versus a declaration. Stay tuned.

There is a spot to fill in what makes you jump for joy! This is about tapping into the playful-child-like wanderlust self. If you cannot think of anything – try remembering what you loved to do as a child! Ask her…you *know* she has an answer!

There are energy exercises (Raising My Exuberant Level) and a ritual-like activity (Magical Moment) to anchor in each day's experience.

There is a fill-in-the-blank for a "How did you D.I.N.G. Today?" (This acronym stands for a Divinely Inspired Non-Doing Guidance-step). The sacred text, *The Tao Te Ching* talks about a concept called *non-doing*. It is described as an *art* in the non-doing, which is not the same as *not* doing anything. Non-doing really equates to allowing. However, there is an active stance to this. This space is just to open up (crack) to possibility thinking. The point of a D.I.N.G. (I really love acronyms!) is that it is a conscious, intentional and on-purpose movement in the direction of your intended manifestation! You move when you are connected and inspired to do so! This is not about trying to make something happen. We've all done that – that's exhausting (necessary sometimes) but that is not what we're doing here. Even if it is left blank, the intention has been sent out into the Universe for that which is yours to do to be revealed. ☺

For example, I set the intention of writing many years ago. I prayed and meditated and ideas for books came to me over time. For example, the book you are holding I began over 7 years ago. I made the commitment to get up each morning at 4:30 a.m. to pray and meditate and then write for one hour. With a houseful of children, this was the only quiet time as everyone was up by 6:00 a.m.! Over the past 7 years other books came to me, which I wrote and 7 of them (hmm…there's a theme on the number 7!) have been published so far. However, this book that you are holding was the result of the very *first* intention I made to write.

I wrote and *allowed* it to simmer over the years. As divinely inspired ideas came, I would add to them. However, I never forced anything to happen. I set an intention. I opened up to receive. I waited until moved to do something. I allowed. But I still made an active stance by getting up, meditating and writing. (Much of what I wrote would be changed or released all together over time to make way for what you are holding in your hands right now).

Lastly, I have created a space for an act of "Conscious Kindness." ***"Kindness is just love with its work boots on."*** *~Author Unknown ~* I had finished this book (or so I thought) and was ready to send it to my publisher, but felt the need to just sit with it for a week. Then, the Conscious Kindness concept came to me. It seemed an appropriate way to end the book and anchor each day's lesson. I love the concept of random acts of kindness. However, I feel many of us have had many hurts along our path that have perhaps caused us to close our hearts. A conscious act of kindness (to ourselves and others) is an intentional opening of one's heart. In this space we will consciously choose each day two ways in which we can be kind. First, we will shower kindness upon ourselves and secondly, to another. I have offered suggestions, as I know when I first started crackin' open space for self-care, kindness to myself was a foreign concept. It was most likely muddled under accusations of being "selfish." I negotiated a new concept. I was being "self-carely." ☺ Hopefully, this will stir your soul to care for you in a way that is unique to you! We are just looking to crack open a little space to let in love (even with its work boots on!).

~

In my work as a neurodevelopmentalist, I learned a lot about how the brain works. The brain integrates information that we take in based on frequency, intensity, duration and consistency. To make changes, we must learn to integrate them into our lives. We get super excited about major changes, but it is often difficult to maintain them – which is probably why most New Year's resolutions are forgotten by February 1. It's not that our wills are not strong – they are *extremely* strong. They are just being driven by something that has *nothing* to do with our conscious intent!

To figure out what that is that is driving us, we need to dig down a little deeper. As we descend into the darkness and let in a *little* light (no need for bright, florescent, non-flattering-revealing-all-flaws-kinda-lighting), we will remember to be kind, loving, forgiving, understanding, and gentle with ourselves.

In the sacred text, *The Holy Bible* it states that the Divine called forth light with the simple and affirmative statement, "Let there be light." Did you notice that there wasn't a question in there, nor was there any confusion about whether or not light existed? It was a simple, declarative intention that clearly there was light somewhere - as in it already existed. The Divine just called it forth into the here and now.

So, as we begin our journey, let us call it forth. Are you with me? So, together we say, "Let there be light!" Oh yeah!

I think I just felt the ground shake!

A compass,
even if adjusted only a few degrees,
over time will land you
in a completely different direction.

Where is your compass pointing?

Things to get for our adventure (optional):

- *White paper, Construction Paper*
- *Gel pens, Markers, Crayons, Colored Pencils*
- *Baking Soda, Lavender Essential Oil, Epsom Salts*
- *$1.00 in Pennies*
- *Pipe Cleaners*
- *Brown Paper Lunch Bag*
- *Seeds (Sunflower or other kind)*
- *Popsicle Sticks*
- *Glue*
- *Cheap Dollar Store Glasses*
- *Wipe Erase Markers or "Write on Glass Markers"*
- *Yarn/String*
- *Stones (Clear and Colored from Dollar Store)*
- *Clear Bowl*
- *Mason Jar*
- *Candles (Colored Small Ones, White & Black Candle)*
- *Things to "Play" with (Described Later!)*

Twenty years from now you will be
more disappointed
by the things you didn't do than
the things you do.
So throw of the bowlines.
Sail away from the safe harbor.
Catch the trade winds in your sails.
Explore. Dream. Discover.
~ Mark Twain ~

Manifest It! Monday

The oak tree began as a
little nut that would not go away.
~ William Blades ~

Day 1

We seem to be in a day and age where something always needs to be fixed, lifted or tucked. Now, I'm not saying I am against looking good and taking care of ourselves – but sometimes it seems it is an all or nothing deal. We're either on a diet or off of one. There have been many reality shows about TOTAL makeovers. I guess a partial makeover just wouldn't get good ratings. But, it seems to me that we didn't arrive to the place we are at in one big makeover moment, so reason says we won't arrive to where we want to be in one big swoop, either.

The concept we will be working with is integration…a little bit at a time. When our higher selves call us forth, we often have to integrate our lower-self behaviors into this new concept. It's kind of like when the power goes out upstairs, you have to go downstairs and flip on the breaker. Or like using a GPS, it often takes many roads to get where you are going and sometimes a re-routing expedition every now and then too! If we want to get anywhere, first we need to know where we want to go, secondly, we have to have some workable directions (broken-down and manageable steps) and thirdly, fuel (inspiration) to get there!

So, the first question we ask is – where do we want to go? We will be looking at areas we can take integrated steps for light-infused living in our: minds, bodies, spirits and self-expression. This book is meant to inspire you on your own path – I share thoughts and ideas that have worked for me and it is my intention that they act as a spark to ignite the passion in you!

Did you know that before lightening actually "strikes" there is a "leader bolt" of energy that makes contact first? What we *see* is the massive charge that runs up from the point of contact to the clouds. It's not the lightening that makes the impact but the *intense charge*. An intention is the "charge" we're exploring and creating today!

So, today – where would you like to let in some light(ening) ☺? Let's begin with some stirring questions to get us started.

We begin by making a list of what we *don't* want. Most often, we learn what we want by finding out very clearly what we do *not* want! Then, next to each *don't want*, right a very clear *do want.* For example, I don't want to gain weight. So, the clear *do want* would be, I *do want* to have a healthy weight.

I *really, really* don't want:	What I *really, really* want!

Now, we're going to look at putting our attention on what we *want* in the form of a declaration. Why not an affirmation? The definition of an affirmation is to state positively and confirm. The definition of a declaration is to make known officially or make evident - formally. The oh-so-subtle difference is that an affirmation is typically that which we are wishing for (usually in the future), whereas a declaration is a statement of fact in the present that we believe to be true.

I have a very unconventional way of looking at affirmations. Let me explain. Having worked as a neurodevelopmentalist, I learned quite a bit about how the brain works. I learned these tools first hand while trying to do sensory integration with my son after his diagnosis of autism. I learned that I needed to do things a little at a time so that his brain could assimilate the input and then integrate it. Otherwise – he went into full freak-out mode!

If we bring information into our consciousness that we do **not** believe or accept on an unconscious level than we can create what is known as cognitive dissonance. This is where our brain is saying…I don't know where to put this as I don't believe what you are telling me. So, basically the new information gets thrown out or made to look like what we already know or believe. We are set up to not allow new information in, so we have to sneak it in the backdoor, so to speak.

Sometimes people hold a core belief
that is very strong.
When they are
presented with evidence
that works against that belief,

the new evidence cannot be accepted.
It would create a feeling that is
extremely uncomfortable,
called cognitive dissonance.
And because it is so important to protect
that core belief, they will rationalize,
ignore and even deny anything that
doesn't fit with the core belief.
~ Frantz Fanon ~

To avoid this, we can provide what I like to call a bridge from what we *know* (and I say this lightly because what we *think* we know is merely based on a belief that may or may not actually be true – but it *feels* true to us!) to what we would like to or have intended to create. I call this an *I C.A.N.!* (These are all done in the "ing" state as it is a continual process of becoming, so it is in the active state always!)

C – Confirming and Committing
A – Accepting and Asserting
N – Negating & Negotiating

1) I am **confirming** what I know to be true (the facts about where I am at) and am **committing** to the *possibility* of a change.
2) I am **accepting** that which I would like to create as a possibility and **asserting** that new possibility in the present in the form of a declaration.
3) I am **negating** any 'disbelief' by **negotiating** a "from here to there place".

It looks like this:

Here: **There:**
(Where I am)   **(Where I want to be)**

Here's an example:

Let's say you want to be at a healthier weight.

1) You will confirm where you currently are. With one caveat. We will add, "Even though…"
   So…"Even though I am not at my desired weight…"

2) While committing to a change, "I am committing to the possibility of a change."

3) Then, you will check in with yourself and find out what is true for you. Ask yourself, "What CAN I believe about this situation? Can I believe that it is possible to be at a healthy weight?" If not, "Can I believe that I can eat less of something or exchange an unhealthy habit for a healthy habit? Can I believe that I can add exercise and if not, what can I believe that my brain will accept as possible?" If you are really struggling with it, you can "tell" your brain "I am open to and believing in the unexpected" or "The unexpected happens." We *know* this is

true because it does (even if on occasion) happen to us, right? This opens a little crack for light to seep in – possibility thinking.

4) You assert that which you want to create in the form of a declaration (it's important to hold the end in mind). That will go in the final cloud. "I am living at a healthy weight."

5) Now, you are negotiating, based on the questions you have asked yourself. So, it might look like this:

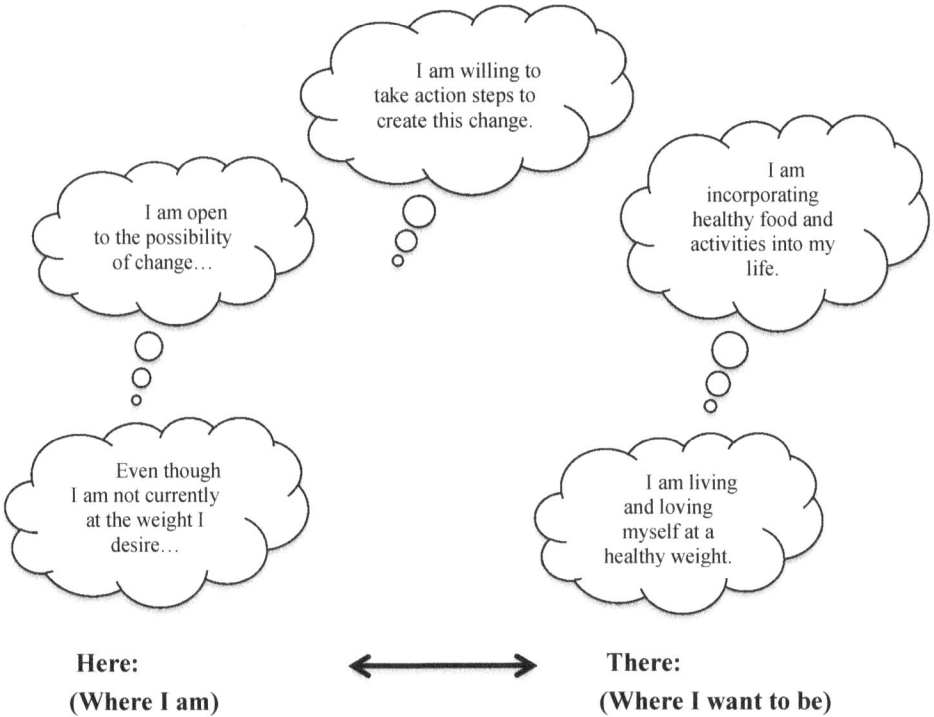

I am willing to take action steps to create this change.

I am open to the possibility of change…

I am incorporating healthy food and activities into my life.

Even though I am not currently at the weight I desire…

I am living and loving myself at a healthy weight.

Here:
(Where I am)

There:
(Where I want to be)

You can even make the statement (beginning to end) "Even though I am not currently at the weight I desire, I am living and loving myself at (or to) a healthy weight."

You can do this with anything you have on your "Do want" list. The goal is to declare this statement as a fact in the now so that vibrationally you are resonating with your desires. If you keep it in the "ing" state, you are declaring that it is in the active phase of becoming - you are not just wishing it into being. This subtle difference will be a signal to your unconscious self to get into an active state of making this declaration true.

If you were to state, "I am wealth and abundance" when you have no money, first of all your unconscious will be like, "Well, if you are – why do you need to affirm it? And oh, by the way – you are NOT!" That's just how our oh-so-black-and-white brains are. I don't know about you, but I typically don't go around affirming things I know to be true. If they're true, well, that's just self-evident, right? However, if you were to say to your brain, "Even though I do not have money in my bank account, I am creating more wealth and abundance opportunities in my life." You acknowledge the reality of your circumstance – JUST NOT ITS PERMANENCE! You are now giving your sub-conscious a "to-do" command.

Something I have learned: I am always intending and affirming. What I have learned is to do this on purpose and move toward what I DO want.

Declaration: I am wide-awake to my good! (You can always add becoming to this, if you are not sure you believe this…"I am becoming wide-awake to my good!)

I Do Declare: _____

_____

_____

7

I am so grateful for: Our ability to choose in every moment how we want to be!

I am grateful for the great: _____

_____

_____

And the not so great: _____

_____

_____

I Jump for Joy when I ….

Raising my Exuberant level: While tapping on the left "fight or flight meridian" (which is located about 2 finger widths above the ear and arches over the ear and down the neck – forming a rainbow), state: "I am no longer…(fearing, believing, creating…) whatever it is you wish to release. For example, "I am no longer fearing that I cannot lose weight" or "I am no longer fearing blocks to my perfect health" or "I am no longer fearing there is not enough." Or, "I am no longer believing that I am not worthy of love." Or "I am no longer giving money all the power." Do this 5-7 times.

Then, while tapping on the right "fight or flight meridian" (which is located about 2 finger widths above the ear and arches over the ear and down the neck – forming a rainbow), you work with your "I am statement." For Example, "I am experiencing my perfect health or desired weight." Or "I am creating enough money." Or, "I am receiving all the love I deserve." Remember to add words if necessary (becoming, moving towards, opening up to…).

My Magical Moment: Today's Magical Moment is brought to you by "How I See Myself In 28 Days!" Write a letter to your 28-day self. Based on the light you are allowing in – where do you see yourself in 28 days? Take some moments to reflect on this, and then add it to your journal…with one twist. I want you to write it as if it had already happened. So, it would look like, "I Am….(enjoying eating healthier, or I am now drinking lots of water...praying/meditating more, loving myself more…"). Remember, we're "ing-ing" - keeping our NOW thinking in the continual and active state of becoming.

If you'd like to make this really fun…draw a freeway (or in my drawing, it looked more like the windy, curvy Highway 1 along the coast of California! – But that's just me…☺). Put a big "*" that says, "You are here!" Then along your road post "signs" of what you intend to see along your journey. As you are doing this, take note of the signs…A *Stop* sign - evaluate – "Is this serving me and my highest good?", a *Yield* sign - "Am I allowing what wants to show up and happen in my life and yielding to its power to transform me?" A *One-Way* sign – "Am I staying on course for where I intend to go?" Don't forget to include a few encouraging billboards along the way ("You Go, Girl!", "You are the best _____, ever!")

Cue *Life Is A Highway* by Rascal Flatts! Let's enjoy the ride, shall we?

D.I.N.G. _____
_____
_____

CONSCIOUS KINDNESS

To thine own self be true... Explore a new restaurant, new coffee shop or new store. Getting out of our comfort zones and exploring novel things not only enlivens us but sharpens our brains too!

Love thy neighbor... Choose one of your loved ones each day this week and do something special for each of them (Bonus: find out their "love language" (just google "love language test" and do something that speaks to them specifically.) Even little notes under their pillows, in their lunch boxes or their favorite "treat" for dessert can bring a smile all the way into their hearts!

At the moment of commitment,
the universe conspires to assist you.
~ Johann Wolfgang von Goethe ~

Treat Me Right Tuesday

The journey of a thousand miles
begins with a single step.
~ Lao Tzu ~

Day 2

Today we talk about energy. The Oxford dictionary describes energy as the strength and vitality required for sustained physical or mental activity. How's your energy level? Do you have the *strength* and *vitality* to sustain your activity level or do you feel like you are draggin' butt? Check in with your mind, body and spirit. How are you hummin'?

If we are going to integrate anything into our lives, we have to talk about energy. Ours, other people's, and all of which we put (or don't put) into our mind, body and spirit. It matters. Matter follows energy. The Tao te Ching describes this as the formless (energy) which comes before the form (matter). We are comprised of energy. Our nervous system is a highly sensitive thirty-seven mile long receptor for picking up energy. It's like a massive lint brush for energy! Yikes! Ever notice how your energy changes when someone enters the room, or you eat something good (or bad) for your body? Whether we are aware of it or not, we are continually picking up energy. Our minds, bodies and spirits are divinely designed to heal themselves. But there are many things (thoughts, beliefs, people, etc.) that can and do interfere with this natural process. Often, we are unaware of many of these. We can get thrown off balance, which interrupts our body's natural healing abilities.

We are looking at letting in a little light into the spaces our bodies open up to speak to us about what is going on vibrationally in our souls.

When I think about energy, I think about water. First and foremost, water, according to scientists, and specifically the process of evaporation, is Nature's most powerful energy source. When I look at water coming out of a facet, it seems so benign. Yet, when I stand by the ocean or view clips from a Tsunami or peer over at the Grand Canyon, I am in awe of the mere force water is and how transformative it can be.

So, in looking at how we transform ourselves energetically, let's look at the properties of water and the process by which water is transformed. First, the properties of water under normal circumstances are: it is fluid (liquid) and seeks its own level; it is tasteless, colorless, and odorless; is transparent; and can act as an acid or base and is considered a universal solvent.

On a spiritual level, the energy of water might look like Divine Love. If I compared water to Divine Love and changed a few words, it would look like this. Divine Love is fluid and goes where it will, has no opinion, with no hidden agenda and is the Universal Solution for any problem.

Water has unique properties of cohesion and adhesion. Cohesion – it sticks to itself (Self-Love) and Adhesion – it sticks very well to other things (Love of others – or like attracts like). Kinda gives a new energetic meaning to the concept Jesus taught, "Love others as yourself."

13

Moving this analogy through the phases of water, in its solid form, Love as liquid moves and flows to where it will. It can be *frozen* where it is hardened and unable to move. Yikes. Yeah. I have felt that kind of "conditional love" have you? There are many times when love comes in the form of expectations (others' and our own), conditions and limitations that keep us *frozen* and unable to move forward. Then there is the gaseous phase of water, which is created with temperature and pressure. Yes, I have felt this kind of Love. It is transformative, for certain. Although it often does *feel* like being boiled. Your soul is calling you forth to move from one state to another.

There is an interesting and rare fourth state called "supercritical fluid." It occurs under rare conditions. It is where water (Love) reaches a critical pressure and critical temperature. Here, the liquid and gas phase merge into one homogenous fluid phase that share the properties of both gas and liquid.

This is the space we are interested in exploring. How do we become more fluid and gaseous? ☺ I'm not suggesting we apply more pressure and temperature. I'm guessing, we're already undergoing that. How do we burn our experience as fuel instead of being consumed by it?

I have been a student of transformation for a very long time. I moved to Phoenix 25 years ago. The Phoenix – a mythical animal that literally lights itself up on fire, burns down and out of the ashes renews itself! Yup. That has been me. In the process, I have studied about alchemy and specifically *spiritual* alchemy. As we are looking at our energy, we will be looking at ways to transform ourselves, vibrationally – from the inside-out. No. We will not be lighting ourselves on fire! ☺

*Changing is not just changing the things outside of us. First of all
we need the right view that transcends all notions including of being
and non-being, creator and creature, mind and spirit. That kind of
insight is crucial for transformation and healing.*
~ *Thich Nhat Hanh* ~

I call today's exercise the ***ABC's of Vibrating Health!***

A – Acknowledge
B – Boundaries
C – Compassion

A - Acknowledge – what do you do (or not do) that affects your energy?
Are you aware *why* you do what you do and *when* you do it?

In counseling people, I have discovered the most powerful tools we have
are our questions. As we gently probe into our being, we discover so
much.

B - Boundaries – do we allow other people's energy to affect us? Do
we set limitations on the energy suckers- food, television, news,
energetic vampires, negative patterns, beliefs, and habits that suck the
life right out of us?

Remember, we're just letting in a little light. To acknowledge and
become aware of where our energy is going is powerful. Pretend your
energy comes in the form of money. Every day you get $1.00. How
much of your dollar is spent on that which you really want and are
intending to "spend" it on? How much gets thrown away or worse,
stolen because we're unaware of it?

C - Compassion – for yourself and others. How much of your energy is spent in the past and in guilt or regret? Can you allow the fluid power of Divine Love to trickle into the spaces that need to be healed?

As we cycle through the phases of Love, much like the phases of a water cycle, we can become more aware of our energy, how fluid we are, where we are "frozen" and where we are transforming.

Something I have learned: Everything is energy. I can become conscious of the energy in and all around me.

Declaration: I am fluid. I am Divine Love moving and having its very being in and all around me. (Remember to add "becoming more" if necessary...)

I Do Declare: _____

_____

_____

I am so grateful for: the ability to choose on purpose that which fuels me!

I am grateful for the great: _____

_____

_____

And the not so great: _____

_____

_____

I Jump for Joy when I ….

Raising my Exuberant level: A beautiful way to clear your energy is to take an "energy bath." Take 1 cup of baking soda, 1 cup of bath salts, a few sprinkles of lavender essential oil (or some bath salts already have the lavender added in) and a little coconut oil, if you'd like for softness – it's slippery, though, so be careful! Add all of it to a warm bath and soak. Light a candle, turn on some beautiful and relaxing music and enjoy!

My Magical Moment: Get $1.00 in pennies. Go through the ABC's and question yourself. Then get a piece of paper and draw little circles and put areas your energy is going. Here are some examples: family, children, friends, work, studying, working out, volunteer work, self-care. Then there are others: toxic relationships, unhealthy habits, television, social media. Just take a look and acknowledge where your energy is going. The "magic" is in the awareness that you get to spend your energy any way you choose and you can always choose differently!

D.I.N.G. _____
_____
_____

CONSCIOUS KINDNESS

To thine own self be true... Go to the health store and explore healthy alternatives to the chemical-laden soaps and body washes we use. There are some delicious alternatives!

Love thy neighbor... Send a hand-written note or flowers to a friend.

You are stronger than you feel-smarter than you think
and more beautiful than you could ever imagine!

There are two ways to live your life.
One is as though nothing is a miracle.
The other is as though
everything is a miracle.
~ Albert Einstein ~

19

How I Wonder & Wander Wednesday

Each day comes bearing
its own gifts.
Untie the ribbons.
~ Ruth Ann Schabacker ~

Day 3

My youngest came to me later in life. There was a ten-year difference between her and her brother. I don't know if it was because I talked to her a lot in utero, or that there were so many adults who were always talking to her but basically, she came out of the womb talking! She wakes up talking and does not ever stop. She even talks in her sleep. She has been talking in full paragraphs since she was two! She can move flawlessly from one topic to another! People always comment about how talkative she is. After doing a neurodevelopmental assessment at the age of four, we were told, "She is linguistically gifted." Hmm…is that what it's called? It does not always feel like a gift (hee hee).

After spending years of negotiating my love/hate relationship with meditation as I could hardly stop the incessant chatter in my head, I had finally found a little quiet space where I could reside. Now, my outside was SO NOISY! ☺

At first, I would fight this. I would be thinking, "I just want 5 minutes to think for myself!" Yet, here was "reality" chatting a mile a minute *in my face!* So, I decided to challenge the thought (that was making me miserable) that I *should* be having quiet time. It certainly wasn't a very "quiet" and peaceful thought and was actually creating a great deal of anxiety for me. When I just melted into her sweet little stories and voice, I fell more in love with her and myself in the process. I could see *me* wanting to be heard and by hearing her (giving away what I myself wanted), I "heard" me too. And as life has a way of flowing perfectly, we would have our delightful conversation and she would be done – moving on and I did get some quiet moments here and there. But I learned to feel the all-encompassing silence within me that could hold me even amidst the chatter. It was within the non-resistance of what was happening in the moment where it finally surfaced. Silence is golden, but true connection (to ourselves and our loved ones) is platinum!

Are you *shoulding* all over yourself? Are there areas in your life that you have an expectation that what is actually happening *should* be different? I wonder if we are able to look into our lives, can we find the space of acceptance that what is happening is supposed to be happening – because it **is** happening. Our unhappiness comes from wanting it to be different. What is causing the discontent is our "shoulding". Although there might not be any particular *lesson* that needs to be derived from a situation, to shed light into a dark corner of *should* might allow us to just put some space around what is happening. We can do this with a simple shift in our own thought process.

I wonder…how might I see this situation differently to have more peace about it?

Where can I drop the "should" and expectation? I can still set an intention but I am opening a little crack to see what **is** happening with less resistance.

Something I have learned: A situation is only ideal if "I-deal" with it. I always have the ability to *choose* differently in my head!

Declaration: I am accepting *fully* what shows up in my life and I can choose peace in this moment - always. (Or…"I am learning to accept fully…")

I Do Declare: _____
_____
_____

I am so grateful for: Non-resistance. I can choose to breathe and flow with my life.

I am grateful for the great: _____
_____
_____

And the not so great: _____
_____
_____

I Jump for Joy when I ….

Raising my Exuberant level: To reframe: hold one hand on your forehead, the other on the back of your head (where the skull meets the spine). While holding, say out loud, "soften and flow", and then "release and let go". By engaging and stimulating the meridian (neurovascular reflex point) you increase the vascular flow through the body, which induces a relaxed state. We process our thoughts and emotions in the frontal lobe (forehead), and the occipital (back of head) is where we hold our past memories and our experiences. This hold allows us to hold our past memories and release them.

My Magical Moment: Here's a *challenge* (and trust me, the magic will be clear and evident!). Take a 7-day "Should-Free" diet. Oh, sorry – I promised no dieting. ☺ For the next seven days (or until next Tuesday) try to catch yourself when you should all over yourself! Make this fun and playful, do the energy exercise above and just become aware of it. Notice the difference in your energy level.

D.I.N.G. _____
_____
_____

CONSCIOUS KINDNESS:

To thine own self be true... Put on an erotic piece of music and move your body in a sensual way! Awaken the sensual part of yourself that likes to move in her own special way!

Love thy neighbor... Pay for someone's coffee or toll behind you in line.

*This we know; all things are connected
like the blood that unites us.
We do not weave the web of life,
we are merely a strand in it.
Whatever we do to the web,
we do to ourselves.*
~ *Chief Seattle* ~

We're In This Thing Together Thursday

Faith in action is love.
Love in action is service.
~ Mother Teresa ~

Day 4

I believe a life lived in service is so fulfilling. You show up in each moment asking how it is you might serve. What it *used* to look like in my life was martyrdom until exhaustion and "angrily" giving of myself. I did not set healthy boundaries. I was raised with the Disease to Please and always said "yes" to everyone and everything and "no" to me while resenting it later. While being completely unconscious of this! I *truly* thought I was giving. But, one day I woke up (in utter exhaustion) and looked at it and realized that this was not really service. It was enslavement to a belief and I had done this to myself, while blaming everyone else. But you CAN change something once you are aware of it and so I did.

We cannot give away what we do not have. We cannot truly love or serve others, if we haven't turned that love onto (into) ourselves.

How are you loving and serving yourself?

True service is not always in *what* we do but the way in which we show up to do it. It might not even have anything to do with anyone else. It can look like *mindfully* packing lunches, folding laundry, picking up a friend's child afterschool or sending a card to someone when they pop

26

into your mind. It is showing up to the mundane tasks in our lives with a loving heart. Now when I make a salad, wash clothes or play ring-a-round-the-rosy *one more time*, I try to do this with a heart filled with love and service. In this moment, it becomes THE most important thing I can be doing. There is only peace in this space.

I feel so drawn to Mahatma Gandhi, Mother Teresa and those who have dedicated their lives to serving others and I am so inspired and have often "shoulded" all over myself that I should be serving in a bigger way. But, service for me takes on the face of a weary mom who at the end of the day, when asked by her child to read one more "extra" story, reads with love and delight (although I do have a 3-book limit at bedtime…I have learned to set healthy boundaries for my service to myself as well!)

Service means showing up heart and all. It also looks like saying "no" to things that I need to as well. Sometimes a soft "no" to someone else is a resounding "YES" to ourselves!

Saying yes is easy – to others. We tend to get this in reverse. We say yes to others and no to ourselves. Let us entertain the notion of correcting this oversight. A good "bridge" from a complete no to yes looks like, "I'm not sure, but let me get back to you", or "Hmm…let me think about it." It buys us some thinking time – not that we need excuses but sometimes we just need to hit the pause button.

We can begin to crack open a little more space for self-love by paying attention to what we say "yes" to and what we say "no" to.

Something I have learned: Only **I** can say yes or no in my life. I do so with great intention of honoring my True Self.

What is your soul asking you to say "yes" to?

_____

_____

_____

What is your soul asking you to say "no" to?

_____

_____

_____

Declaration: I am saying yes and no with great clarity and love. (Or…I am learning to say yes and no…)

I Do Declare: _____

_____

_____

I am so grateful for: The ability to give from an over-flowing, never-ending abundance that I can always connect with.

I am grateful for the great: _____

_____

_____

And the not so great: _____

_____

_____

I Jump for Joy when I ….

Raising my Exuberant level: Here's a fun exercise. Learn what "yes" and "no" feel like energetically in your body. There are two ways to try this. First, stand up. Cross your arms over your chest like you are giving yourself a big hug. Now, state something you can say "yes" to, like, "My name is…." and state your name. See if your body moves forward or backwards. Now, state something that you can say no to (you can use the same question, but say a different name that is not yours). See if your body moves forward or backwards. Play with this. You can also do this sitting down and notice any sensations in our body that would indicate a yes or no. Play with this for a while. Sometimes we are unaware of the subtle nuances within our bodies, so it takes some time to notice.

My Magical Moment: Draw a picture of yourself. Now, put a circle around yourself. With arrows going toward yourself, what are your healthy boundaries? Write them in. Now draw a dotted line around yourself. Recognize ways in which you are not currently setting healthy boundaries (or saying "no"). Write those in as well. Loving ourselves starts with healthy boundaries – oh yes!

D.I.N.G. _____

_____

_____

CONSCIOUS KINDNESS

To thine own self be true... Have a "say yes" night. This is say yes to pleasure, fun, goodness, compliments, someone else taking the lead...

Love thy neighbor... Let someone go ahead of you in line, or offer to help someone with his or her groceries.

You are stronger than you feel-smarter than you think
and more beautiful than you could ever imagine!

I get up every morning determined
both to change the world and to have
one hell of a good time.
Sometimes this makes planning the day difficult!
~ E.B. White ~

Fun, Fun & More Fun Friday!

Some people play in the rain.
Others just get wet.
~ Roger Miller ~

Day 5

Fridays we are working with the idea of FUN! This is about connecting to that little girl inside who wants to play and loves exploring what makes her soul vibrate with joy! J.O.Y. (Jumping Out of Yo'self!) If you can, find a picture of yourself when you were little – any age will do. I think twelve was a magical age because we were not still little girls, but not yet grown women. It's also an age where many of us lost ourselves. Let's ask her what she'd like to do. Go ahead…she's probably been waiting for years to hear from you!

Today make time for you to go play. Take yourself on a shopping trip – go to the store (the Dollar Store is great for this!) and gather up the following Girly-Girl Survival Kit (and please feel free to add/delete as it serves your inner Goddess Girl!)

- Fun basket or container to keep all of your treasures (and you will need to hide them! These are yours and your kids will be all over this!)

- Coloring book & crayons (and not the ones left over from your kids!) Any color mediums that speak to you.

- Print (off of the Internet) mandalas or buy a book of them. You can order them online if you can't find them in a bookstore.

- Playdough or clay.

- Paints and a big pad of white paper (or a journal)

- Your own unique "self" stuff (for instance, if you like to design houses, magazines, or a software program that will allow you to do this, or Legos), if you like to design clothes – Barbies and outfits.

- Something you really wanted as a child, but never got.

Put on some playful music *(Unwritten, Free, What a Feeling, This Girl is On Fire)*. Have fun exploring who you are and who you want to be (when you grow up! ☺) Even if you only take ten minutes to honor your playful side, you'll be amazed at how much lighter you feel.

Can you sneak in a 10 minute swing at the park?

Does your local mall have a merry-go-round?

Can you go fly a kite?

Could you rent *Pollyanna* or *Mary Poppins* or a fun movie to watch? (My personal "go to" is the original *Charlie and the Chocolate Factory* (coupled with a dark chocolate bar!) or the original *Footloose*!)

Ironically, this day might end up being the scariest. We become very good at lists, "to-do's", self-improvement, diets, house remodels, and meeting everyone else's needs. To stop and truly unplug and reconnect to just *being* can be the most challenging thing we ever do. But it becomes the most important thing we ever do. If we do what we've always done, we'll get what we've always gotten.

I live in Phoenix and about an hour and a half from Sedona. I used to think I had to go up and spend the night which prohibited me from going so many times. I finally figured out that I could grab my hiking shoes and go for the day! It was liberating that I could *integrate* this amazing experience into my life!

Want something new? You are going to have to *play* by new rules. Emphasis on PLAY!

I _____ commit to more play in my life! I am so freakin' worth it!

This is how I'd like to integrate fun in my life:

_____
_____
_____

Something I have learned: Life IS fun and delicious – I am going to jump in with both feet! You can't get wet from the *word* water! You're gonna have to jump!

Declaration: I am honoring the little girl in me.

34

I Do Declare: _____

_____

_____

I am so grateful for: Playtime! Play is our "work" for the day!

I am grateful for the great: _____

_____

_____

And the not so great: _____

_____

_____

I Jump for Joy when I ....

Raising my Exuberant level: Sometimes our energy gets jumbled up and is headed backwards. To correct this, we'll do something called a Thymus Thump, massage our "energy buttons" and do a cross-pattern march. 1) Make a fist and while saying "ha, ha, ha", knock gently on the space in the center of your chest. 2) On both sides of your collar bone there are two fleshy "pads". Massage both of these with your index and middle fingers for about 30 seconds. Breathe. 3) Now march in place, while touching your right hand to your left knee as it comes up, and alternating with your left hand on your right knee as it comes up. Do this for about 1-3 minutes.

My Magical Moment: Today we're going to make an Inner-Goddess Warrior doll. Take a pipe cleaner, cut it in half. Now, bend one of the halves in half again and twist it to make a circle (the head). Now fan out the bottom two pieces to make feet. Now take the other half of the pipe cleaner and twist it around the body to make arms. Each night share your fears and wishes with this doll. Place it under your pillow and say:

> *This doll represents the inner warrior-goddess in me.*
> *The part in me that has often had much to say but has fallen*
> *silent over the years of heaviness –*
> *some from others, some from myself.*
> *This doll reminds me that at my core*
> *I am resilient, beautiful, flexible and strong.*
> *I AM LOVE!*
> *As I strip away all of the layers that are NOT me,*
> *I find her. I honor her. I remember her.*
> *I AM her.*
> *She reminds me to never forget. I can speak to her of my fears*
> *and she will carry them onto the wind where all the goddesses*
> *whisper back to me of my strength and courage.*
> *I speak to her of my dreams and together*
> *we make them a reality.*

D.I.N.G. _____

_____

_____

CONSCIOUS KINDNESS

To thine own self be true... Honor the "Inner Sexy Goddess" in you and explore new scents, sensual massage oils and sensual clothing. Tap into a part of yourself that longs to express more sensuality.

Love thy neighbor... Buy an old-fashioned toy (jacks, jump rope, coloring book & crayons, a loom – remember those? etc.) for one of your girlfriends – honor her little girl or even better...treat you and her to a playdate!

Turn your face to the sun and
the shadows fall behind you.
~ Maori Proverb ~

My & My Shadow Saturday

The elixir is hidden
in the poison.
~ *Rumi* ~

Day 6

Here we look into the shadow, to crack open any beliefs that have kept us from living our best lives. Ask yourself the following question: Do I deserve to have abundant, exuberant happiness in **all** areas of my life: love, health, prosperity, and creative expression? Could I handle being filled with joy and peace in all of these areas in my life? Which one caused a little lurch in your stomach when you tried to feel it – or make it your own? Today, let's begin with love.

Love – to what degree are you able to receive love? A good way of knowing is looking at your relationships with others. A *great* way of knowing is looking at your relationship with yourself. This is where we find out how "deep is your love, is your love – how deep is your love…"

Take a moment to get quiet and breathe. The following can take a few moments or lots of moments. Make sure you honor yourself by allowing enough time and quiet to do this authentically. We're dropping off some bags and some bags might be heavier than others. Be gentle, loving and kind with yourself through this. It's ok to break this down into smaller steps, also. Remember, we didn't get here overnight. It's all right to take some time – as much as we need to heal. We're just crackin' open a little. The Light will do the rest.

Do you feel worthy of love – yours, others but also love from something greater than yourself? Can you see yourself in Divine Light as whole and perfect and in need of no changes to be loveable? If not, ask yourself when you stopped feeling unconditional love from something greater than yourself? We came here with it – do you know when this belief started? Be still and wait.

Do you have a picture or an incident that created this belief? Go back and look at it. See yourself and the other person involved in this situation. If no picture comes to mind, view your childhood. Was it happy? Were you safe, happy, and unconditionally loved? If not, where does that feeling of unlovable-ness or not feeling safe resonate within your body? *The following does in no way excuse any wrong that happened to you by another person.* What we want to do is shed light on this so that this situation is **no longer** wounding us. In order to do this, we have to look at the situation differently. We are "re-viewing" (as in viewing again) this situation, only with different eyes in order to heal. This is **not** for the other person. This is for US!

In this situation, ask yourself, "What would I have needed in this moment to feel whole, healthy, and loved?" Create in your mind what *you* would have needed (to be held, hugged, loved, listened to and validated instead of hit, abused, neglected, yelled at or _____).

Stop. Breathe. Now, give this to yourself. To do this, picture your adult-self-giving to your "little girl" self what YOU needed at that time. This can be a specific incident or just in general. See her, get down on your knees, hold her hands and tell her you will never leave her and YOU are here to protect her – now and always. See her smile!

You can create this new memory of healing for yourself. Send beautiful, healing, Divine-white-light to the part of your body that "felt" this pain. You can do this as many times as you need to. You are "parenting" yourself now from a healthier, safer, and more loving place. YOU are re-creating you. You are loving yourself from a higher place. Crack. You are letting in some light.

Ultimately, to heal we must let go and FORGIVE. We want to GIVE up the pain FOR something greater – healing. It's ok if we are not ready to do that right now. It is a process as we first REVEAL our pain, FEEL it, then DEAL with it and ultimately HEAL it. **Reveal. Feel. Deal. Heal**. This is not releasing anyone else from the responsibility of what THEY did. We just no longer want to carry the pain of what they did inside of **us**. We want to crack it open, let in light into a part of ourselves that is still casting shadows in our present-day happiness, take back our power, give ourselves what we needed and let love in. Once we look at something through the lens of Truth, the healing can begin.

Something I have learned: When I pull myself out of my past, I can enjoy the present…it is a gift I give to myself!

Declaration: I am safe. I am loved. I am healing. (Or…I am feeling safer or more loved each day…)

41

I Do Declare: _____

_____

_____

I am so grateful for: The past – for it is created who we are right now and we are Divine Perfection!

I am grateful for the great: _____

_____

_____

And the not so great: _____

_____

_____

I Jump for Joy when I ….

Raising my Exuberant level: Do you know you can equip yourself with an "Auto-correct?" And not the bad kind like your smart phone – mine is always auto-correcting me straight into embarrassment! ☺ When a shadow part of yourself comes up whether it is in the form of a negative thought, a derogatory thought directed at yourself or others, or a pattern you have repeated, you can auto-correct it. There are several ways to do this. The first way is to smile. Like a big, goofy-grin-all-the-way-down-in-your-belly-smile! Then try tickling your lips (this engages the parasympathetic nervous system). Then focus on something and conjure up as much gratitude for it as possible (I've done this with broccoli! It's hilarious and I feel so silly – but that's the point…it changes my vibration from low to high!) Lastly, talk to yourself as if you were a little child with a boo-boo. Be tender, kind, understanding and sympathetic.

My Magical Moment: Get a piece of paper and draw a timeline of your life. Review significant times in your life. See if you can find hidden beliefs (about yourself and the world) along the way. Place Band-Aids on places you are still healing and write on the Band-Aids – "I love you. It is safe. We are healing."

Now go back and look at the timeline. See if you can see where something in the future was causing the "past" to happen. Let me give you an example. I grew up in a small town and probably would have stayed there forever, as my other family members had, except I married young and my husband was finishing school in Columbus, OH, so we needed to move there. We later divorced, but the point is, it moved me out of my comfort zone. I eventually landed a job where I met the "future" father of my two eldest children. If I look back on my timeline, I can see the future pull of my children in creating my first marriage that could have looked like a 'mistake" as it ended in divorce, but it was a mere stepping stone to get me where I needed to go. I would have never moved on my own. I have many, many of these. If I tried to explain to you "why" I was divorcing when I was divorcing, I don't know that I would have had an explanation except that I *knew* I had to. I can now look back and the answer is obvious.

See if you can identify those stepping-stones in your own life. See if you can see how it was all necessary and part of the process of getting you where you needed to be. This is not about trying to make up meaning. It is about facilitating a greater understanding (which hopefully helps us now when we undergo situations we do not understand) of all of the stops along life's highway.

D.I.N.G. _____
_____
_____

CONSCIOUS KINDNESS

To thine own self be true…Treat yourself to a massage or a pedicure. If you are on a budget, there are typically massage schools close-by that offer discounted massages.

Love thy neighbor…Whenever you or a family member gets a new item (clothing, toy, etc.), give a similar item away.

Sorrow has its reward.
It never leaves us
where it found us.
~ *Mary Baker Eddy* ~

*A Zen master said to a monk, "You must see the universe
in your cup." The monk looked into his cup, but didn't see
the universe, so he threw the cup away. The Zen master
said, "Oh, poor cup. We think the cup is too small to hold
the universe. Intellectually, we can't see how it could
fit. But wherever we go, the whole universe always
appears--in a cup, a window,
in a smile, in a word."*

Sacred Serenity Sunday

It's like driving a car at night.
You can never see further than your headlights.
But you can make the whole trip that way.
~ *E.L. Doctorow* ~

Day 7

Let's look at our sacred selves. Do we feel connected to something greater than ourselves? Do we connect to that Source regularly? Can we, by faith, drive through our lives merely by seeing just what is out in front of us at the moment? What is your source? What do you believe in? This crack is about looking at what we truly believe versus what was handed to us. Most of us were given answers before we asked any questions. Would you agree that the Source is unconditionally loving? Yet, how often do we (and those who have helped us formulate our beliefs) place conditions on the love we give and receive?

I was raised to believe in a God that was conditionally loving, at best, and down-right punitive when you did something to earn *His* (if I am made in the image and likeness of God, why is he a *male*?) disapproval (as when I divorced). When this happened in my life, I had to "break-up" with the God of my childhood as it certainly had a lot of conditions on the love offered. Crack. A little light came in. My love and devotion to a higher power didn't shrink – it was finally able to expand into the spaces of *real love*. But I had to crack open and let out the erroneous beliefs that were handed to me. The kind of love that sees all, bears all, hopes all, endures all and can heal all (yeah – even *those* places). My experience allowed me to expand to let in more light. I realized that Spirit/Source/Energy – whatever you want to call that which is greater than us, grows our fingernails and loves unconditionally needs nothing from me. It is complete – an endless ocean of love that we can swim in, drink up, bathe in and it never runs out. It is always flowing to us wherever we are at, lifting us up, and washing over us and through us like an all-encompassing, engulfing hug. It brings only peace, true joy and contentment. No shame, no sadness, no lack of worth and absolutely no conditions.

Do you see yourself as sacred? Can you connect with a Being that loves you exactly as you are, right here, with no conditions?

How do you define this power greater than you?

_____

_____

Something I have learned: I do not have to do anything to earn the love of Spirit/Source/higher power/God – or whatever I choose to call "it". It is always present for me – I just have to be open to receive it.

Declaration: My Source's love is unconditional and washes over me.

I Do Declare: _____

_____

_____

I am so grateful for: The power of unconditional, healing, never-ending, all-encompassing love. YOU are loved!

I am grateful for the great: _____

_____

_____

And the not so great: _____

_____

_____

I Jump for Joy when I ….

Raising my Exuberant level: Go outside in your bare feet. Stand tall with your naked feet on the earth and your hands over your heart. Feel the invisible connection you have with "the web". Whatever or however you define your connection, see it, feel it and know it is there. Feel your feet firmly on the ground as if you have roots shooting out of the bottom of your feet all the way down to the core of Mother Earth. Now with a great big breath open your arms up to the sky. Breathe in all of the wonder, bliss, magic and energy the Universe has for you. Do this each day and feel your vibration expand.

My Magical Moment: We're going to make a tree. Take a brown paper lunch bag; lay it flat (unopened), and cut ½ strips from the top (opening of the bag), nearly to the place where the crease is. On each strip (which will become your branches) write ways in which you wish to branch out in your spiritual practice. Now, take the bag, open it and write on the base of the bag the spiritual practices that you have right now that ground you. Now twist the middle section of the bag and twist the ½ strips to make branches. As you begin to see manifestations of your intentions and spiritual practices, add leaves to your tree.

D.I.N.G. _____

_____

_____

CONSCIOUS KINDNESS

To thine own self be true... Go to the library or bookstore and browse for a title that is not your usual read – open and discover something new!

Love thy neighbor... Send a letter or gift to a child you know...they so love getting mail!

Love moves into places we have left open –
Even just a crack.

We have completed our first week! Reflect here and congratulate
yourself for all of the work that you have done thus far. Your light is a
little brighter and you're crackin' yourself up! ☺ It may feel raw and
rugged right now,
but you are braver than you have been told,
stronger than you have believed,
smarter than you think
and more beautiful than you could ever see!

Hum along with me…

"This little light of mine…I'm gonna let it shine…"

50

You are stronger than you feel-smarter than you think
and more beautiful than you could ever imagine!

To turn yesterday's dream
into tomorrow's success,
we must act today.
~ Unknown ~

Manifest It! Monday

Every day is a new opportunity
to ask more questions
and see what happens.
~ Elizabeth Wurtzel ~

Day 8

Who would you be if you were not you? If you could re-define who you are right now, who would you be? What would you do if success were *guaranteed*?

Did you know that that there are more cells in your body than there are stars in our galaxy. There are 75 – 100 trillion cells that comprise your body! Just in reading that sentence 25,000,000 have died. Every 7-10 years you have a completely new body. Our cells respond to everything that we think! The good news is that we can literally "think ourselves anew!" We are not "stuck" with the being that has been created by our erroneous beliefs. We can re-think ourselves into who we want to be! Whew! Doesn't that feel great!?

But, I think along our journey we need to clarify *why* we are improving ourselves as much as how. As a co-crackee (yes, we're in this thing together!), there are aspects of our lives we want to change because they no longer serve us. We know this by what we are currently getting out of life (that we do not want). While making these changes, however, we must hold onto the Truth that we are perfect and WHOLE just the way we are. This seems contradictory, but we always want to hold in mind love, compassion, and acceptance as we move through our changes. We are all divine creations and Spirit says so – to you, to me, and to the goofy lady down the street ☺! We just might be believing (be living?) a story about ourselves that needs to be re-written in that truth.

Our first step towards excavating our best is finding out what that is. To do this, we must talk to the expert – ourselves. Buy or borrow (or dig out of the bottom of a drawer somewhere 'cuz I'm sure someone bought you one for Christmas sometime) a journal or a notebook. Each day do some random writing – preferably when you wake up. We're not talking a novel, here – just random ramblings (and rantings, if you prefer). We just want to wake the sleeping giant within. Ask yourself, "How do I want to live my best life?" then let it roll…every day just for 10 minutes – turn on the facet! I left my notebook in the bathroom – it seemed a good place to *release* unwanted stuff from my life!

Most of what I wrote at first seemed like nonsense, but over time, it worked to unplug the cork because the creativity began to pour throughout the rest of the day and weeks to follow this. I realized I was tuning into my long, lost voice. This is an extremely powerful exercise. It's great to ask a question and see what flows out from yourself as the answer. Oh, and here's a tip – do not go back and read what you've written. The wisdom isn't necessarily in what you've written, but in what you **will** write. You are just letting go, unleashing your voice and allowing it to find a platform in which to speak! Livin' out loud…that's what we're doing!

53

Something I have learned: There is no part of me that is not perfect – only parts that have been hidden from the healing light of the Divine.

Declaration: I am whole and perfect and finding my voice. (Remember to add "becoming" if you need to…)

I Do Declare: _____

_____

_____

I am so grateful for: Beauty that resonates from within and radiates outward.

I am grateful for the great: _____

_____

_____

And the not so great: _____

_____

_____

I Jump for Joy when I ….

Raising my Exuberant level: To keep from getting stuck in the past while writing about it, "Ground yourself" periodically. To do this, when you feel un-centered, immediately name 3 things you can 1) see, 2) smell, 3) hear, and 4) feel. Take a deep breath in and out slowly three times.

My Magical Moment: I used to periodically burn up what I had written in my rambling/ranting records (I told you I liked fire!) It's fun to do this and then scatter the ashes on the sidewalk outside your door. Then making a "clean sweep" – sweep them up and toss them. Then, write your life as a Fairy Tale. With one caveat…write it from reverse. Take a moment of pain (perhaps the one you might be undergoing right now) and make it the pivotal moment – the turning point in your story. "I, so cleverly designed this magical alchemic moment of ….. (fill it in) so that I could …"AND THAT IS HOW I CREATED A LIFE WORTH LIVING AND LIVED HAPPILY, EUPHORICALLY EVER AFTER!!

D.I.N.G. _____

_____

_____

CONSCIOUS KINDNESS

To thine own self be true…Take a nap today – even if for only 20 minutes! Learn the art of power-napping and honoring our need to "regroup" and restore!

Love thy neighbor…Volunteer to read at a hospital, classroom or homeless shelter.

Affirmations are like prescriptions
for certain aspects of yourself
you want to change.
~ Jerry Frankhauser ~

Treat Me Right Tuesday

*Sometimes things fall apart
so that better things
can fall together.*
~ *Marilyn Monroe* ~

Day 9

In physics, if you want to see how something *behaves*, you have to make it uncomfortable and see what happens. Yeah. I've experienced this, have you? Until recently, the second law of thermodynamics has stated that **all** physical processes in the universe inevitably fall apart. Oh, this is good news, now isn't it – what!? Seriously!! That basically, things flow from order to disorder. Yeah, that has happened a time or two in my life – how about you? ☺

However, recent discoveries (and oh how I love me some new discoveries!) suggest that certain materials, under *particular circumstances* might counteract these laws and come together instead of fall apart. Oh yeah. That's what I'm talkin' about!

I'm quite interested in those particular circumstances. Are you?

One of the first turkeys I made for Thanksgiving was a disaster. It looked so beautiful. It did not have one of those pop-up thermometers, so I called my mom and asked her how to check if it was done. She said to use a meat thermometer (they make those!?) Anyway, I actually had one – it must have been a wedding gift or something. So I put it in and

57

nothing was happening. She said, "You have to push it in very deep. You want to check the internal temperature of the turkey. That's what counts."

Not that we want to compare ourselves to a turkey. ☺ But, how much time do we spend "dressing the turkey" instead of checking the internal temperature of our being. One more diet, makeover, or workout regimen is not what we're talking about here. We've all been down this road. I did a Google search and found 24 new diets – yeah, *new* ways to punish ourselves in addition to the hundreds of old ways! Yet, 69% of people over 20 are overweight and 35% are obese. Clearly, the "new" or old for that matter, diets are losing ground, not pounds. It is because being healthy is an inside job! It starts with a commitment to our whole being. In crackin' up old beliefs, patterns and thoughts that no longer serve us, we want to look at our internal temperature.

Health – where would you like to be? And remember, we are looking at ourselves in new light – with love, gentleness, kindness and understanding. What does an optimal state of health feel like? (Hint: it is not a number!) Setting aside pounds for now (haven't they weighed us down long enough?) and focus on what we can add to our well-being plan to be healthy.

Take a moment to stop right now and breathe. Breathe deep into your belly for a few moments. Now check in with your body. What is one area you know you would like to make a change? We usually know what we need to do. Our body and spirit usually are whispering to us (sometimes it becomes a loud roar, too!)

My approach to my health was about adding in something good as opposed to depriving myself of the things I had become used to. When I wanted to ultimately eliminate diet soda, sugar and white foods from my diet about fifteen years ago, I began by adding healthy alternatives a little at a time. First, I replaced a white bagel with a whole grain one (I am now gluten free totally, but this process of integration took some time but really worked for me!) I also wanted to drink more water, so I just got a 20- ounce water cup from Starbucks and committed to drinking 1 of these each day (in addition to the other liquids I was consuming). I now drink about 3-4 of these each day. For example, if you are looking to integrate healthier drinks and are currently drinking 5 sodas a day, what does it feel like to eliminate and/or replace 1 with something healthy? (PS – there is a great alternative soda that I have enjoyed called Zevia. It is all natural and sweetened with the natural sweetener, Stevia and actually tastes very good!)

When we are moving from what we used to be to who we want to be, we need a little bridge to cross over. Remember, on day one how we talked about cognitive dissonance. It is what happens in our brains when we cannot integrate the unfamiliar –our brains are literally freaking out saying, "Where do I put this? I don't know what to do with this…AHH!" So, we calm this incessant chatter with a sneaky system called integration. When my son was in the throes of autism, he refused to eat vegetables. So, I "integrated" (o.k. hid!) them in his pizza sauce. Eventually, as we did sensory integration (hmm…is there a theme here!?), he would eat the real, unmasked version of the vegetables. I just had to convince his brain that he could let it in. Remember. Crackin' up. Letting in a little light. Emphasis on little.

Get a piece of paper and make a list of foods that 1) Raise your vibration, 2) Foods that are neutral (neither raise nor lower your vibration) and 3) Foods that lower your vibration. See if you might negotiate some healthier versions of foods you really like that are lowering your vibration.

So…ready!? Get out your red pen, girl! This just got real!

I _____

(Your name – Your Goddess name, if you prefer!)

Commit to ME – to be healthier because I SO deserve life's BEST in all ways, in the following ways:

_____
_____
_____

Something I have learned: I no longer punish myself for not being what I *think* I should be. I love myself unconditionally NOW – just the way I am.

Declaration: I am becoming perfect health. All the cells in my body KNOW this truth and resonate with love and light.

I Do Declare: _____

_____
_____

I am so grateful for: YOU! You are a beautiful miracle – there has never been, nor will there ever be anyone quite like <u>you</u>!

I am grateful for the great: _____

_____

_____

And the not so great: _____

_____

_____

I Jump for Joy when I ….

Raising my Exuberant level: Remember a time when you were super-duper happy – almost giddy-like?! Now describe this moment to yourself as if it were happening right now. As you "see" this in your mind's eye, place a pink bubble around it. Pink is associated with love and the heart chakra. Now, with this feeling-state activated in your mind's-eye, bring into the pink bubble your intention (that you just wrote above). Hold this for about twenty seconds!

My Magical Moment: What would you like to integrate into your life? You will need a plain piece of paper, yellow construction paper, a Popsicle stick or pipe cleaner and seeds (any kind - sunflower seeds, popcorn kernels if you really want your intention to "pop"!) and some glue. On the Popsicle stick write "I intend to …" Now, take the yellow construction paper and cut out sunflower leaves. On each leaf write your intentions. You will glue this and the Popsicle stick on the piece of paper. Gather the seeds, hold them in your hand while repeating your intentions. Now – "plant" them with glue into the middle of your sunflower. Place this where you can see it each day!

D.I.N.G. _____

_____

_____

CONSCIOUS KINDNESS

To thine own self be true…See if your local community center or community college offers dance classes – how about belly dancing? Minimally, find a YouTube video on belly dancing and move your hips! I've heard they don't lie. ☺

Love thy neighbor…Share a favorite new healthy find with a friend or your child's teacher…share the love!

Most people see what is
and never what can be.
~ Albert Einstein ~

How I Wonder & Wander Wednesday

One does not discover new lands
without consenting to lose sight
of the shore for a very long time.
~ *Andre' Gide* ~

Day 10

Did you know that hawks and birds of prey, even though they have eyes smaller than humans have vision that is eight times more acute? Could it be their perspective is better than ours? Perhaps our limited view is just a lack of perspective.

My son was obsessed with tall buildings throughout his years struggling through autism. He would want to go to the top floor to see everything. Maybe he intuitively knew that if we were going to ever solve the enigma of his autism, we would need to take it higher – way higher! I believe our spiritual journey is analogous to this. It seems my perspective on the first floor of my journey was limited – by only what I could see and touch. As I grew into greater awareness, as in moved up a few floors, my perspective grew as I was able to take in much, much more.

I wonder…how much do we miss in life because we are looking at all the wrong things? How much do we misinterpret because the lens by which we view things is faulty, limited or just plain fogged up? I wonder what it would be like to just take one area of our lives and view it differently. What if we could just take it higher?

Right now, as I write this, I have one month before I will be seeking a new source of income. This is not the first time I have been in this place. But it is no less disconcerting. I feel all of my insecurities screaming at me and I want to curl up in a ball. So I first stop the incessant chatter in my head by taking a deep breath. I then envision this fear as if it had a color, shape, and texture and move it visually out of my body in front of me. Unfortunately, my "fear" doesn't have a shape and feels much like an endless void. I want to wrap my arms around it to carry it away, but I don't seem to be able to grasp onto it. I decide it will be ok to allow it to just hover near me as I move toward my imaginary elevator. We both negotiate the space inside as I feel its presence but sense a little space between us now. I close my eyes. I breathe.

The elevator begins to move. We ascend up. I breathe. The doors open. I step out, feeling a little bit lighter. My fear follows me. But it is, if ever so slightly, a bit smaller. I realize it might not completely dissipate. Then a thought occurs to me. Maybe it is here to help me move on. Hmm… I feel the fear shrinking. Maybe it is not really fear at all. Maybe it is just uncertainty. Shrink. I then wonder if this uncertainty is where I will allow light in to illuminate where I will go (grow?) next. Shrink. I look at my new "friend" or at least "non-foe," and realize everything I feel is just an opportunity for me to move past where I currently am at. It has come not AT me, but FOR me…to crack open a little more for there is more light to be had here. I think I shall call it Freddy (seems appropriate from the horror movies of my past...heehee). But recognize that just as the movie was fake, so is my fear. Freddy and I shall continually negotiate a truce. But I can see my way around it now. As I continually moved toward love (fear's arch nemesis!), it seemed to fade even more!

65

I wonder where could we adjust our lenses for a new perspective? What shall I take in the elevator with me?

Something I have learned: How things "are" truly are a matter of perspective and I can always see them differently.

Declaration: I am seeing with wonder all that is before me.

I Do Declare: _____

_____

_____

I am so grateful for: My inner vision – to see all things clearly.

I am grateful for the great: _____

_____

_____

And the not so great: _____

_____

_____

I Jump for Joy when I ….

Raising my Exuberant level: Lightly place your fingertips on your forehead, covering the "Oh my God" points (the place where your forehead protrudes and located directly above your pupils). Put your thumbs on your temples next to your eyes, breathing deeply. These neurovascular holding points affect blood circulation. By softly holding them for 3-5 minutes you can increase the blood circulation to this area and the whole body. This is a great stress reliever and can give us the ability to release, let go and see things a little more clearly!

My Magical Moment: With your Marker that writes on glass (or sticky notes) – go around your house and write your intentions all over the place – or write a manifestation: I see clearly! Walk around your house and tilt your head (or look at things upside down if you are feeling brave!). Try to change your perspective in any which way that you can. Or take a trip to the tallest building in your town. Ride the elevator "up" with your intentions in your hands and your glasses on – to see clearly and take it all "higher!"

D.I.N.G. _____

_____

_____

CONSCIOUS KINDNESS

To thine own self be true... Ask for a "night off" this week – find a way to play (go make a piece of pottery – or find a group meditation, or a wine/painting class, or just take a walk around your neighborhood alone!)

Love thy neighbor... Offer to give your partner a "night off" this week and invite them to do something fun for themselves.

*I honor the place within you in which
the entire universe dwells.
I honor the place in you, which is of love,
of truth, of light and of peace.
When you are in that place in you,
and I am in that place in me.
We are one.*

We're In This Thing Together Thursday

We must be the change
we wish to see in the world.
~ Gandhi ~

Day 11

Today we explore our significant relationships. You know the ones I'm talking about. There is always that *one* person (our partner, friend, co-worker, or relative) who is just a thorn in our side. Put simply, we "endure" them, not enjoy them (or at least some aspect of them). I'm inviting you, if only for today, to view the relationship as if whatever irritated you the most about this person was a mirrored reflection of you (I hear you yelling at me…stay with me on this one…☺). Breathe.

Who gets under your skin? Or more importantly, what are the qualities about that person that really irk you? Write them down. Look at them. Let's pretend that this person shows up exactly as they are *supposed* to (or we could fight the reality with an idea of who they "should" be, but we've tried that and that's really not working for us, is it?) They are consistently showing up as themselves and they have totally perfected that, now haven't they?

I knew someone who I thought was extremely selfish. It was so annoying and rubbed me the wrong way. I (in my oh-so-high opinion of myself) was a very giving, sharing, caring, blah-blah-blah person). I had decided THIS was the way to be in the world and that being selfish was wrong. (In my defense, it is good to be kind, caring, loving BUT…)

Crack. Here's where love seeped in and infused a little light. What the other person mirrored back to me was my own fear of my being selfish. I had been "groomed" that it was NOT ok to take care of myself. Hear me loud and clear – it is ok to be selfish. It is more than ok, and as a matter of fact necessary to take care of one's self in a healthy way. Because that is certainly no one's responsibility but mine! Loving one's self allows us to set healthy boundaries (for ourselves and others) and also does not inflict our own emptiness on those around us with some ridiculous expectation to "complete us" and/or fill us up. We have to self-care if we desire to fill up our own cup so that we might spill out onto others. As Iyanla Vanzant says, "My cup runneth over. What's in my cup is mine. What spills out – is yours!" Unconditional love must start with us.

We have invited and attracted others into our world so that we might heal. It is a perfect opportunity to let in light. When we feel uncomfortable about an aspect someone is reflecting back, let us examine it a little closer and see if we can't find some way in which we either do something similar and judge ourselves about it or reject this part of ourselves completely. I have found that when my buttons get pushed, and they are *my* buttons, I have found a crack that is ready for some more light.

Who in my life have I invited to teach me something about myself?
(As I say a silent blessing of thanks/gratitude to them)

_____

_____

_____

71

What lesson of love (and the lessons are always kind and loving although at the time, they might not feel that way) could I learn from this? _____

_____

_____

This is about shedding some light into a darkened corner of our soul. There is no need to "do" anything (unless your soul compels you to do so). We are merely looking at this with fresh eyes. Dee Hock said, "Change is not about new things or new ideas; it's about seeing old things with new eyes from different perspectives." (Or from our different selves).

I have a little acronym that I use when someone who is getting under my skin comes into my consciousness. It is FLBR (pronounced *Flubber* – ever see the Robin Williams' movie, Flubber…that big thick gooey stuff that was out-of-control – went wherever it wanted and took over the lab?) Yeah…seems an appropriate name for unwanted thoughts that can take over my brain and get out of control – taking me with it! It stands for **F** – Forgive (no, not Fling…stay with me thoughts!) **L** – Love (what!? Yes, I feel your resistance thoughts – but what we give away is what we give to ourselves…aren't we done flingin' anger, hate and unforgiveness all around?) **B** – Bless (they have been a teacher for us – whether we like the packaging the little gift of the lesson came in or not – I'm sure that we have learned something – even if it is what we do NOT want), and **R** – Release – oh yeah…let it go. That one, we can do. With an open heart…that FLBR is so outta here…taking all of the messy residue with it!

Something I have learned: I have no control over other people – only how I respond to how they "show up" in my life.

Declaration: I am continually creating healthier relationships - especially with myself. I am accepting myself and others – just as they are. (Or I am willing to accept….).

I Do Declare: _____

_____
_____

I am so grateful for: Your precious self! YOU are so worthy of great love!

I am grateful for the great: _____

_____
_____

And the not so great: _____

_____
_____

I Jump for Joy when I ….

Raising my Exuberant level: A lot of times we are bound to someone through anger and frustration – even more so than to people we are connected to in love. You can do an etheric-chord cutting ceremony. Light a white candle and visualize yourself and the other person in your highest-self capacity (which for me involves us in white and "up" in my mind's eye). See the chord that connects you to them. See a beautiful crystal sword that is held by your guardian angel or any angel of your choice (any Higher Vibration being that you connect with). See the two of you thanking one another for the lesson (good, bad or indifferent as it may have been), blessing one another, and then with both of your permission, this chord is cut. Release the other person into Love because knowing that what we give to the other, we give to ourselves. Then, silently bless the situation for the purpose it has served each of you. See it done. But more importantly *feel* it done as your energetic level rises.

My Magical Moment: If there is someone you would like to do a little FLBR with, get some string (or yarn). "Place" this person (this can be done with a thought, feeling or belief also) in a chair across from you. Tie the string to the chair and as you think of all of the ways in which you are "tied" to this person, wrap yourself up in the string. When you are sufficiently *bound* up, stop. Now as you move through the FLBR process, cut away these ties. When you are completely free, burn the string or cut it up and throw it away.

D.I.N.G. _____

_____

_____

CONSCIOUS KINDNESS

To thine own self be true... Buy yourself your own special mug for tea, coffee or lemon water. Find something that speaks to you – that is beautiful and sacred!

Love thy neighbor... Forgive someone a debt...never bring it up again.

I don't want to get to the end of my life
and find I have lived just the length of it.
I want to have lived the width of it too!
~ Diane Ackerman ~

Fun, Fun & More Fun Friday!

Say what you will about the Ten Commandments,
you must always come back to the pleasant fact that
there are only ten of them.
~ H.L. Mencken ~

Day 12

WARNING! WARNING! WARNING! FUN IS HIGHLY ADDICTIVE – PROCEED WITH CAUTION! ☺ OH, AND THERE IS NO **WRONG** WAY TO HAVE FUN!

Fun is really about your ability to experience freedom. Here's a "fun" acronym:

> *F – Freedom*
> *U – Unleashed*
> *N – (in the) Now!*

Find a place where you are alone (I know…this is tricky – it might have to be when everyone is "distracted" ☺). Put on your favorite music (or even better – a tune from when you were in high school!) Sing and dance with reckless abandon. If you can do this at night – with glow sticks – even better! Dance like you are on fire and connected to your True Self!! Make a playlist – of songs that make your heart soar. Music is so powerful. I have several playlists: I call them Play 1, 2 and 3. I also have ones named Happiness 1, 2 and 3. While you are at it, make a playlist that is called Serenity – this will be songs that move you and allow you to "soak" up peace, while in the bathtub, or out in nature somewhere. Take the time to choose consciously what you are going to fill your mind with. It matters.

After you have giggled yourself silly – go to your toy box and find something fun to do. I am so hoping by now you look forward to this day and give yourself "permission to play." If not, take today to wander through the toy store (without your children is advisable ☺). What calls to you? Where did your inner child get stunted? What does she wish to play with? Maybe you really need to kick it up and join a kick-boxing class, or a Salsa dance or belly dancing class – or rock climbing. It is NEVER too late to be what you have always been! If you don't know, ask your little "you" – they know!

As we are playing around here, check in with yourself and see what are your personal, "rules of engagement?" Do you have some "commandments" you live by, either on purpose - or default)? I love the line in Pirates of the Caribbean where they describe the *rules* as more like guidelines. Yes. That feels good – there seems to be some wiggle room in there. For "fun" (yes, finding out about how we play, why we play in a particular way (or don't) is FUN (freedom unleashed in the NOW, right?). Because we cannot change something we are not aware of. Make a "Playlist of your life". Which includes what your Life Commandments and or Guidelines are. Do any of them need to be altered or banished completely? Is there *freedom* here? It's kind of hard to play if one of your commandments prohibits you from doing so? See what I mean? ☺ Just a small crack. Ahh…feel the warmth of the sun coming in?

Something I have learned: I can be free to experience fun no matter what I do. It's always a choice.

Declaration: Fun is my birthright. I can play with reckless abandon. To play is to honor my true self.

I Do Declare: _____

_____

_____

I am so grateful for: Play!

I am grateful for the great: _____

_____

_____

And the not so great: _____

_____

_____

I Jump for Joy when I ....

Raising my Exuberant level: Name the following (as quickly as possible and without looking it up on your phone!): The last 3 American Idol winners, the last 10 people who won the Nobel Peace Prize, the last

4 teams who went to the Super Bowl, the last five winners of the Miss America contest, and the 3 wealthiest people in America. How'd you do?

Now, try this: Three people who "have your back" at every turn, your favorite teacher, someone who has made you feel loved and appreciated, someone who taught you something invaluable, and a hero story that inspired you.

The people we learn from, who raise our vibration are those who impact us directly. Make sure you are *playing* with people who raise your vibration way up!

My Magical Moment: Trace your hands. Now, on the left hand, draw or write your past (memories, thoughts, feelings, beliefs, situations). Then, on the right hand draw your future. Where do you want to go? To make this super-duper fun, you can do this in Plaster of Paris. As you look at one or both of these, do you have a mission statement for your life? If you did…what would it say? Play around with it and write it on the back of the hand! ☺

D.I.N.G. _____

_____

_____

CONSCIOUS KINDNESS

To thine own self be true... Can you sneak in 10 minutes of play somewhere today? Can you have a beauty treatment done? Look on websites like Groupon to find a coupon for a treatment at a spa – then schedule a spa day (you can do this alone or with a great gal pal!)

Love thy neighbor...leave a generous tip next time you get coffee...like more than the cost of the coffee! ☺

Build a future –
Don't just polish the past.
~ Unknown ~

Me and My Shadow Saturday

The most dangerous lies are
those that most resemble the truth.
~ Unknown ~

Day 13

H – HAVING
E – ENOUGH
A – ALL-CONSUMING
L – LOVE
T – TO
H – HEAL

Health begins with our beliefs about what we deserve. Can we really receive the unconditionally (truly NO conditions) love of the Divine in all areas of our lives? We are often punishing our own selves for something someone else did or said in the past – as if we picked up where they left off. We do this because we haven't learned how not-to-do this, or simply are unaware we are doing this. Crack. We can cling to something because it feels safe and familiar, not necessarily because it is serving us. We have never really questioned the opinion others had or have of us to see that it is perhaps their own stuff projected onto us. Where might the body be holding this punishing memory for you? Do you have an ache or pain that just won't go away? While struggling with the decision to divorce, I had a continual stomach-ache. It got so bad, that I had acid reflex to the point of perpetual laryngitis. I literally lost my voice. A wise friend asked me, "*Who* in your life can't you stomach?" Crack. The decision became clear and I "healed" nearly instantly. (I also listened to my body, did some research and found natural supplements to re-establish homeostasis in my body but the decision to honor myself and feelings resonated throughout my entire body, activating the healing energy within).

Get very quiet. Ask yourself, "What do I need right now to be whole and healthy? Is there someone, or something I am holding onto, a belief I am no longer resonating with or some part of me that is desiring a change?" Now listen. We learned the process of inquiring into our subconscious for a "yes" or "no." Ask your intuitive-knowing-self if it will cooperate with you and reveal the answers to these questions.

Healing is an inside job. I have a visualization I do for myself each day. I do this in the shower, because – that is when I think of it and it makes sense there. I visualize divine, loving energy in the form of masculine on one side and feminine on the other. The feminine energy has green light pouring out of open hands into the top of my head, while the masculine energy has pink, loving energy pouring out of open hands into the top of my head. It washes over me (as I'm showering you can see how this makes this visual is so powerful). As I wash myself, I imagine removing any energy, thoughts, patterns or beliefs that do not work for me (I don't even have to acknowledge them individually), I just allow them to wash away collectively. I see them go down the drain. Then the last rinse is a ray of beautiful white light coming down into the top of my head, pouring over my entire being. I then cover my body with Coconut Oil (I put nothing on my body I wouldn't put in it!) that "seals" in this Divine love, light, power and protection! Voilà – clean, mind, body and spirit!

You may or may not have heard about chakras. Chakra means *wheel of energy*. The 7 major chakras are subtle gates for energy (called Prana or Ch'i) to enter. The chakras transform energy from the subtle words of pure consciousness into the dense physical world. Each one has a location, a specific purpose, and emotion. There are many ways to balance these subtle energy bodies as well.

A simplified explanation of the seven chakras is: The Root Chakra is located below genitals, is about survival and the emotion is fear. The Sacral Chakra is located above the genitals, is about relationships and the emotion is desire. The Navel Chakra is located at the solar plexus, is about desire, inner strength and the emotion is anger. The Heart Chakra is located in the middle of the chest, is about love and the emotion is also love. The Throat Chakra located in the throat area and is about speech and the power of communication. The Third Eye Chakra is located between the eyebrows and is about intuition, awareness and insight beyond the five senses. The Crown Chakra is located above the crown of the head and is about higher consciousness, corresponds to our higher selves and is about the power of consciousness.

Each chakra is connected to our human awareness. When we have blocks in our chakras, they can create mind-body-spirit issues. The five lower chakras are related to our physical body functions while the sixth chakra relates to our mind's higher mental functions and the seventh chakra relates to our spiritual consciousness.

We want to open up to receive healthy, healing energy. The left side of our body is considered our feminine side. It is open and receives energy.

Our right side of our body is our masculine side and sends out energy into the world.

Our chakras can be balanced in many ways. A vocal toning exercise is located at the "Raising my Exuberant Energy level" section at the end of today's lesson. It is a great exercise to do while in the shower or car!

Below is a chart for a few ways to balance the chakras:

Chakra	Main Issue	Food	Smell	Stone
Root	Grounding/ Security	Protein	Cinnamon	Hematite
Sacral	Relationships Emotions	Liquid	Dragon's-Blood	Coral
Navel	Will Power	Grain	Ginger	Amber
Heart	Love	Veggies	Heliotrope	Kunzite
Throat	Communication	Fruit	Eucalyptus	Turquoise
Third Eye	Awareness Intuition	Pure Air	Lavender	Lapis
Crown	Consciousness Spiritual Love	Fasting	Jasmine	Clear Quartz

Something I have learned: I, and others can only give away what is inside. If I am full of love, I have it to give away. I can only be full of love if I allow myself to receive it first.

What area of your body is asking you to pay attention to it? What does it want to say? Ask it.

Declaration: I am continually perfecting my health. Divine light, love and joy permeate my entire being. I send divine, healing light to _____ of my body.

I Do Declare: _____

_____

_____

I am so grateful for: perfect health!

I am grateful for the great: _____

_____

_____

And the not so great: _____

_____

_____

I Jump for Joy when I ....

Raising my Exuberant level: Use the following chart to "sing" through the chakras. You can use the familiar tune of "doe, ray, me, fa, so, la ti..." (hopefully, you have seen the *Sound of Music*!) while using the sounds listed.

Chakra	Sound	Note
Root	Uh (like up)	doe
Sacral	Ooh (like moo)	ray
Solar Plexus	Oh (like so)	me
Heart	Ah (like law)	fa
Throat	I (like hi)	so
Third Eye	Aye (like play)	la
Crown	Eee (like see)	ti

You can use this fun little song I made up if you would like:

THE "IT IS SO" SONG!
(To the tune of "Do, Ray, Me Fa, So La Ti")

Uh, I stand here in my truth
Ooh, create what's mine to do
Oh, I open to receive
Ah, I love myself and YOU!
I – speak what is mine to say
Aye – seeing clearly every day
EEE – connected to my Source

And I know that IT IS SO! So, so, so…
(repeat as often as your heart desires!)

My Magical Moment: Draw, make out of string, or rocks or make a sand tray with one (or you can download one from the Internet) a labyrinth. Laminate it (you can use clear contact paper to do this). When you feel stuck on something, think about the "problem" and then trace your way into the labyrinth with your finger. As you hold this energetically in mind go all of the way to the center. At the center, see the "problem" resting in the center. As you wind your way back out, feel that the resolution to the problem is winding its way to you now. I've made one out of Dollar Store rocks. You can hot glue gun them to cardboard, decorate it and use it during your meditation.

D.I.N.G. _____

_____

_____

CONSCIOUS KINDNESS

To thine own self be true... Buy or make a chakra bracelet to remind yourself to stay in balance! Sing your chakras clear in the shower or in the car alone!

Love thy neighbor... Volunteer to babysit for a single mother so she can get out and play!

Anything in life that we don't accept
will simply make trouble for us
until we make peace with it.
~ Shakti Gawain ~

Sacred Serenity Sunday

We have a choice to plow new ground
or let the weeds grow.
~ Plowed Ground ~

Day 14

What does meditation look like to you? I have negotiated a relationship with traditional meditation on and off for about 20 years. I often felt like I was swimming up-stream. Quieting my thoughts? Ha! I could barely quiet my household, let alone my thoughts! Although, I can now achieve a few moments of silence – strung together, I understand that my thoughts are not really the issue. It is my belief in them that causes me grief. Ahh…sit with that "thought" for a moment.

I love watching children play. When my youngest daughter was three, she would kick a ball, and then that became a forum for a different kind of play, which led her over to the sandbox which evolved into something else and back and forth and on and on and it seemed so random and chaotic. Yet, when I would step back there was a flow and rhythm to it that was beautiful. This becomes my view of my thoughts. I step back and observe them flowing here, there and everywhere. Sometimes, it's quite amusing and I laugh out loud! If a thought arises that makes me hold my breath or feel all clammy, I can breathe deeply and say, "It's just a thought – I can believe it and feel uncomfortable or I can let it go. What's my choice?"

It's analogous to weeds to me. I don't know about you, but I have never planted a weed – ever. Yet, they are everywhere in my front lawn! They just pop up out of nowhere. Now, I have planted flowers (our affirmations and our "intentional" thoughts would represent flowers in our mind-garden!) and I nurture those and they grow beautifully. But, the weeds – the only thing I can do is pluck them from my garden. (Or I can choose to leave them – the reality is I get to choose and that is a good thing!)

It's ok to choose the weedy thought (leave the weed in the garden) – however, we're just shining some light in the darkened corner of our mind. Crack. We're acknowledging it AND our choice to pick it or leave it. This allows for some "space" around the thought – so that the thought is not in charge – **we are** – the highest part of ourselves.

For some, meditation has a goal – no thought. That is an admirable goal. But sometimes just observing our thoughts can be insightful (as in…what *do* I think about all the time?) Noticing. Do I have a weed or a flower? We ponder the thought. Interesting. Either way, we are recognizing – it's just a thought. Good or bad. It will pass.

Our mindful meditation then becomes observing the thought. Seeing it written on a "cloud" in our mind and passing through. Then, for mere moments, we might glimpse the sun. When we do, we take in the warmth. And when the clouds roll in, we wait. For we know in mere moments, the sun will peak out again.

One form of meditation I have enjoyed is Japa (or mantra) meditation. It involves using a saying (affirmations are good!), or a prayer or recitation that speaks to you. For example, if we were to use the affirmation on the next page, we would "see" it written in on an imaginary white board in our mind's eye in vivid color (ooh...I'll choose red!). We then take a deep breath, recite the first word out loud. Then, we notice the second word and if but for a moment, "breathe" into the little space between the two words. A moment of silence, if you will. Then you move on to the next word. You continue this throughout the entire recitation or affirmations. It would be great to keep a list of your affirmations and use them during meditation – kind of a 2 for 1 deal! ☺

Something I have learned: I may not control my thoughts, but I can decide if they control me – or not.

Declaration: My thoughts are just thoughts. I am watching my thoughts as they pass through me. I can choose to believe this thought – or not.

I Do Declare: _____

_____

_____

I am so grateful for: the ability to choose.

I am grateful for the great: _____

_____

_____

And the not so great: _____

_____

_____

I Jump for Joy when I ....

Raising my Exuberant level: Buy or make prayer/meditation beads. It is great to use these during meditation (touching a bead while repeating your declaration). Then you can wear your declarative statement all day long!

Something else you can do is a SaTaNaMa Meditation. While making the Sanskrit sound "Sa", which means birth, you will touch the tips of your thumbs on both hands to the tips of your index finger (it makes a little circle). Your index finger represents knowledge and the ability to release limitation. Then, you move to the sound "Ta", which means life, while making a little circle with your thumbs and middle fingers. Your middle finger represents patience and wisdom. Then, while making the sound "Na", which means death, you make a circle with your thumbs and ring fingers. Your ring finger represents vitality. Lastly, you make the sound "Ma", which means rebirth, while making a circle with your thumbs and little fingers.   Your little finger represents clear communication. Repeat this mantra throughout your meditation.

My Magical Moment: Take a piece of string (pink – love, green – prosperity, yellow – willpower, red – security, blue – to release sadness – the "blues") and tie it to a tree or bush while saying, "When the ribbon flies free, _____ comes to me." See it blowing in the wind to bring to you that which you intend.

D.I.N.G. _____

_____

_____

CONSCIOUS KINDNESS

To thine own self be true... Buy yourself a flower or plant!

Love thy neighbor... Smile at everyone you encounter today!

Each time you act in spite of your fear,
you discover even greater, deeper courage.
~ Art Berg ~

Manifest It! Monday

Knowing who I am took some time.
Finding out who I may become
will take a lifetime.
~ Linda A. James ~

Day 15

When I was potty training my daughter, we bought those wonderful new inventions (they did not have these when my older children were potty-training), called Pull-ups. I thought – how clever – like a diaper. The only problem was that they did not allow her to "feel" what it felt like to be wet. Now, it said it did that – but for her, it did not work. So, I went back to my tried and true method – a bunch of big shirts and panty-free for two weeks! Now, we had a few "wet carpet" moments, but this allowed her the opportunity to FEEL what it felt like to be wet and ultimately what she needed to feel in order to know when she had to go potty. We eventually moved to real panties and all was well.

I think sometimes our life lessons are like that. Stick with me on this one. Sometimes we walk around not able (or wanting) to *feel*. We have our vices that keep us from feeling – from toxic relationships, incessant busy-ness, alcohol, food, social media (yeah…you know who you are! ☺ - no judgment). It's ok that we have those – because we do. But we just want to shed a little light (panty-free anyone?) here. Just a slight acknowledgment – even if it's a half-nod tin the general direction of the "doing." We can then look just beneath it and see what we are running from.

Most of us have spent most of our lives covering up, hiding from and masking our feelings. A lot of us were told, "Don't you feel and for God's sake – don't talk about it!" I locked my feelings away as a child and didn't unlock them, or was even aware that I had done that for many years into my adult life. Enter children into my life and bam! I was starting to react (over-react?) to their feelings and realized I might have an unhealed festering wound or two in their somewhere. This isn't about blaming our parents. Most of them are wounded children too. We all do the best we can, where we are at, with what we are given. I was angry at my parents for a while and it was ok – even though I get why they did what they did, it hurt me. It's ok to acknowledge that. Then move on. Being told you do not feel a certain way (when you do) or not being allowed to feel what you feel (when you feel it) can really disconnect your head from your heart! So, we want to re-activate or shine a little light onto those feelings. It's a start. Because it is when we *feel what we feel* that we can begin to heal.

While you move about your day and your life. Take a moment to just hit the pause button and check in with how you feel. You don't even have to label it if you do not want to. Just start by asking the question, "What do I feel?" You will begin to light up the part of you that remembers what it is like to feel. Try checking in at least morning, noon and night. Check in with your body, also. Where am I holding this feeling?

Bring your feelings into the Light. Love will meet you there. Actually, Love is already there.

Something I have learned: My feelings are non-negotiable! I feel what I feel. They serve as a temperature gauge for where I am at. Am I feeling angry? Where am I incongruent with what I say/do and what I *want* to say and do? I acknowledge my feelings without judgment.

Sit quietly and ask yourself. What am I NOT really feeling? What feeling scares me the most?

Declaration: It is safe to feel my feelings.

I Do Declare: _____
_____
_____

I am so grateful for: the ability to feel. My feelings signal to me where I am at.

I am grateful for the great: _____
_____
_____

And the not so great: _____
_____
_____
_____

I Jump for Joy when I ….

Raising my Exuberant level: Buy some loofah gloves and a small ball (about the size of a tennis ball). We're going to use this to create sensory awareness. First, taking the loofah gloves, for two minutes each day, rub your arms and legs. Then, follow it up with rolling the ball with a small amount of pressure up and down your arms and legs. This deep pressure awakens your sensory system and provides necessary input for feeling. Try this on your partner and kids. It feels so great. It is a tool we used to integrate sensory stimulation for our son who was having a difficult time *feeling* when we were moving him through autism.

My Magical Moment: Try to really *feel* everything today. Touch your plants. Put your feet on the grass. Run your fingers through your children's hair (if they'll let you!). Pick up your food and intentionally touch it, taste it, feel it in your mouth. Open up to the different textures around you and really take it all in. You can also try a sensory meditation. Here you can use either a food (a piece of juicy fruit is great), music, or even a warm bath. Take the time to allow your senses to really "take in" the entire experience. Become complete aware of the whole experience using all of your senses.

D.I.N.G. _____

_____

_____

CONSCIOUS KINDNESS

To thine own self be true... Buy a blank mask (the Dollar Store is great for things like this) or make one from paper. Write words that describe your True Beautiful Self!

Love thy neighbor... Give your family members a shoulder massage.

The only way to discover the limits
of the possible
is to venture a little way past them
into the impossible.
~ Arthur C. Clarke ~

Treat Me Right Tuesday

Wherever you go,
no matter what the weather,
always bring your own sunshine.
~ *Anthony J. D'Angelo, The College Blue Book* ~

Day 16

Now that we are working on one thing to integrate into our perfect healthy being, let's look at support for that work – our thoughts. Our thoughts arise all by their little selves. We don't control them anymore than we control our breathing (although we can direct our thoughts – some arise completely out of nowhere). They truly have a mind of their own. Simply put, we do not have the ability in our minds to tell which thought is true and which thought is not true. The popular belief is that we have over 70,000 thoughts per day (there is a debate about the accuracy of this number, but Deepak Chopra supports this belief, and well, I trust him! ☺). A lot of the thoughts we have each day are repetitive – as in, we continually "rethink" the same thing over and over.

Can you remember a time you had a thought and it felt so real and you were *certain* it was correct - but it turned out to be wrong? It happens to us all the time – the problem is we don't know it at the time. Many of our thoughts are based on beliefs that were created in the past and we have simply never challenged those beliefs (or often have not even been aware of them!) So, we essentially, rethink the past into the now each and every moment and that past may or may not be grounded in our current truth (or any *real* evidence for that matter!) So, what can we

103

do? Well, first, we can ask ourselves if the thought we're having is *really* true. When I say *really,* I am asking where is the current evidence? Sometimes we want the truth – sometimes we do not. By simply posing the question, we are open to the possibility that the thought is not 100% true. By doing so, we can open a small crack for a different perspective.

Another way to deal with recycled thoughts is to formulate a new thought in the form of what we *want* (not what we do not want) or simply be open to the possibility of a new thought. For example, if you catch yourself thinking the thought, "Nothing good ever happens to me" or when something bad happens, "This *always* happens to me!" You can pause by asking yourself where is the evidence that supports this thought or more importantly where is the evidence that supports a different thought. We can then provide a bridge from the old, recycled thought to a new and improved thought!

We can also take our thought up a notch. I have a visual of myself entering a crystal elevator with my current thought. There is only one button in this elevator and it is labeled "higher." I push that button and feel myself ascending (with my current thought). For example, let's say I put on a pair of jeans that are too tight and my critical self starts a barrage of not-so-nice thoughts that can quickly descend to down-right nasty thoughts – all sucker-punching my self-esteem and self-worth. These can be recycled thoughts from my past or my present. Yes, it sounds ridiculous, but we do it and it happens oh-so-fast that we are often even unaware of the damage! I jump into my imaginary elevator (tight-won't-button-up jeans and all) and hit the button. Up we go. It allows me to reach for a different thought. Now, I can stop on the first floor, where the thought might *look like*, "Well, I am a little bloated. Whatever." Then, off come the jeans and I move on. Or I can go even higher, "I have been eating a lot lately, I wonder if I'm stuffing my feelings. How can I love myself more and listen to what I need to do?" or even higher, "I am so loveable. Just the way I am. I see myself with love and compassion and know that I will be guided to and directed to all I need in all ways."

Tight jeans are just well, tight jeans. Elevating our thoughts about everything allows us to see thoughts just as they are. We might reveal things along the way that need to be healed. But we must first put a little space around our thoughts.

Something I have learned: I can determine what kind of "thought food" goes into my head. I am conscious of what I read or view.

Declaration: I am deserving of perfect health, wealth, love and creative expression.

I Do Declare: _____

_____

_____

I am so grateful for: The courage it takes to make change!

I am grateful for the great: _____

_____

_____

And the not so great: _____

_____

_____

(Optional – Create several affirmations (remember to provide integration or a "bridge" when necessary) and post them everywhere & carry them around with you!)

I Jump for Joy when I ….

Raising my Exuberant level: As you are holding in mind a "recycled thought", place your hands on the top of your head, directly above your ears, so that the end of your palm is touching the top of your ear. Hold and press for thirty seconds. Feel and "see" yourself squeezing out the negative thought (or thoughts) to make room for a new thought. Breathe. Release it and then place your hands on the very top of your head in a "V" formation. Visualize and state out loud the new and improved thought. *Feel* it coming in through the top of your head!

My Magical Moment: Recycle those thoughts. You can get some dissolvable paper (order it online if you like) or use paper that is already available to you…toilet paper ☺. Separate the sheets and "write" down things you would like to release. Flush it down – figuratively AND literally! You can also create circles out of white paper. Write down a thought you would like to recycle on the circle, crunch it up and throw it away in the recycle bin!

D.I.N.G. _____

_____

_____

CONSCIOUS KINDNESS

To thine own self be true... Stop what you are doing throughout the day and take a break – even if for a moment to deep listen to yourself. Breathe. Say 5 nice things to yourself about yourself!

Love thy neighbor... Deep listen to someone...with your whole being!

Some stories don't have a clear
beginning, middle and end.
Life is about not knowing,
having to change,
taking the moment and
making the best of it,
without knowing what's
going to happen next.
Delicious ambiguity...
~ Gilda Radner ~

How I Wonder & Wander Wednesday

Mama exhorted her children to
"jump at de sun."
We might not land on the sun,
but at least we would get off the ground.
~ *Zora Neal Hurston* ~

Day 17

My daughter's father is a daredevil and coerced me (yeah, I was a chicken) into doing some pretty daring things while we were married. Although our marriage had it difficulties, this is a gift he gave to me that I will always be grateful for. He helped me to excavate and cultivate my inner playful self! On one trip to the Cayman Islands, we went in a Bubble-sub under the ocean and on the same trip parasailing. I had never done either. Talk about facing my fears. One down below with no air and one up above with nothing *but* air! But, the parasailing took my fear to a new level. Literally.

Now, I'm not really afraid of dying – or at least so I thought until we strapped in and started going higher and higher. Finally, we climbed to about 800 feet. The wind catches the parachute and the contraption (which is a harness that basically feels like a swing) begins to lurch. It makes a funny (and I don't mean ha-ha funny) sound. My stomach starts doing somersaults. I am feeling incredibly vulnerable. Now, prior to this trip I had been seeing a lot of turtles. I lived in Florida at the time, and I rescued one from the middle of the road. Little did I know that I was about to become a turtle...as my life was about to dramatically change and I would literally be trying to create a home of my own. I looked up the meaning of a turtle and it meant "Mother Earth, adapting to new surroundings, trusting your inner wisdom." I was going through a lot of changes and quite frankly, not trusting myself (or anything for that matter) at that time. I had seen many turtles already on this trip— under the ocean in the Bubble-sub, we saw three of them and our guide said he had never seen so many).

So, while I'm flying high, feeling my fears (and not just about flying – my whole life was changing and fear was screaming loud in my face!), I closed my eyes and said a silent prayer. I opened my eyes and saw an enormous sea turtle! I was warmed from the inside out. I felt supported, held, heard, and oh-so-validated in the moment. The ride ended with a little dip in the water and I felt a little braver for having flown. I knew it was symbolic of my life unfolding, and I felt a sense of peace.

As I moved through a divorce, I faced many fears – aloneness, having three children (my youngest was only 3-years-old at the time), my son looking to home-school the next year due to social problems from some lingering traits of his autism, I had 1 year to finish my degree and had been home with my children for 16 years. I had supported one husband through school and a thriving career and helped another build a successful business – but had no employable skills or assets to show for my years of support, dedication and stay-at-home status. I was staring some pretty big fears down. But, it was all good. I knew Spirit was in all of it. My theme was "Leap and the net will appear." I did a lot of leaping (and sometimes it felt more like being shoved!) And quite frankly, there were times I felt like I was hangin' ten a little longer than

I was comfortable with, but the net always appeared (or on occasion, I was even able to fly.)

When you look into the face of fear, what do you see?   Sometimes we don't want to look. That's ok. We look when we are ready. Sometimes, it is a while after we look before we actually do anything. That's ok too.

Do you know how baby eagles learn to fly? Their mother pushes them from the nest. Just about the time they would hit the ground, she swoops down and catches them and then the whole process begins again.

What would really push you out of your nest? Do you trust the Mother God energy that is in and all around you to swoop in and catch you?

Without thinking, answer the following as quickly as possible:

I feel…
I wish…
I think…
I need.
I hope…
I want…

Something I have learned: If I have a choice between love and fear (and I *always* do), why would I choose fear? Maybe I didn't know I was choosing – by default…hmm…

Declaration: I am feeling my fear – and doing it anyway.

I Do Declare: _____

_____

_____

I am so grateful for: opportunities to learn how to fly!

I am grateful for the great: _____

_____

_____

And the not so great: _____

_____

_____

I Jump for Joy when I ....

Raising my Exuberant level: As you hold in mind a fear, with your right hand, grab the top of your left shoulder muscle and squeeze. Take a deep breath and as you release the breath, turn your head away and look over your right shoulder. Inhale as you return your head to the center. Then exhale as you look over your left shoulder (while still squeezing the left shoulder muscle). Inhale as you return your head to the center. Then exhale as you drop your chin to your chest. Do this three-5 times. Then repeat with the left hand on the right shoulder.

As you are exhaling, visualize your fear being released. As you are inhaling, visualize a renewed strength and connection to Love and peace.

My Magical Moment: Make a Wishing Well. Take a large clear bowl and drop different colored candle wax on the bottom and then adhere a white candle on that spot. You can choose a different color for the different things you wish to manifest (green for prosperity, pink for love, yellow for health, blue for peace, etc.). Each morning light the white candle and throw a coin in the bowl as you make a "Grateful Wish" - a gratitude (giving thanks in advance for that which you *wish* for and/or grateful for something that has already shown up in your life). If you want to really anchor it, take a coin from your wish well and toss it into moving water or plant it into rich soil.

As your gratitude wishing-well grows in abundance, consider taking the coins and doing a random act of kindness or giving the money to a special charity that speaks to you.

D.I.N.G. _____

_____

_____

CONSCIOUS KINDNESS

To thine own self be true... Say to yourself, "Today, I completely love and accept myself. Just the way I am." Feel free to repeat this often (and daily).

Love thy neighbor... Compliment other women today – let them know they are beautiful! We all SO need to hear this!

There are two lasting bequests
we can hope to give our children.
One of these is roots.
The other is wings.
~ Hodding Carter ~

We're In This Thing Together Thursday

A child's life is like a piece of paper
on which every person leaves a mark.
~ Chinese proverb ~

Day 18

Today we talk about children – ours, other people's, or just children in general. So even if you do not have children – play along. For how we relate to children often reflects our own beliefs about ourselves.

I was blessed with two amazing bonus kids, Stephanie and Kevin (I met them when they were ages 2 and 4 and consider them "my own"), before I birthed my other two children two years after having met them. We lived in the same town as them briefly. However, when my youngest son (Kenton) was 2½, my husband's job moved us to Arizona away from Stephanie and Kevin, which was very difficult and painful. It was revealed as necessary, when Kenton was diagnosed with autism at age 3 ½ and all of my energy and efforts would needed to be directed towards his recovery while still being a Mommy for his older sister, Alexis. When Stephanie turned 13, she came to live with us in Arizona. Ten years after Kenton was born (and fully recovered!), I had my precious Riley.

If there is one thing I know about kids – it's that they crack you! Something you think you know "for sure" is cracked wide open when you have children. You become extremely raw and jagged.

I have tried to keep in mind a few things while raising all of these children ☺. One, they are on loan – they have come *through* me, not *to* me. (I lovingly refer to myself as "the tour guide"). They are NOT mine and I am being entrusted with them for their guidance and instruction for a few years, but ultimately they have to learn their own lessons here in life. They will struggle (only if I allow them to, by not always choosing for them and loving them enough not to rescue them continuously from their consequences). My job is to give them plenty of opportunities to make decisions for themselves in the safety of an environment that supports them, encourages them, loves them unconditionally, and mirrors back to them their True Selves. Most importantly, I want to make sure I am working out my own issues and not asking them (even if unconsciously) for them to carry the burden of my "unfinished" business.

In my work with many families, parenting issues seem to come to a head during the teenage years. Our baby birds have wings and they are not afraid to use them (sometimes all over our faces!)

So, today we take an honest look at our relationships with our children (or those in our immediate environment). How are they working? Are they loving (unconditionally), do I have safe, healthy boundaries for my children AND myself? Can my child come to me with *anything* – honestly and know that I will love and accept them through it? Have I resolved my issues or are they interfering with me parenting my child on purpose and in peace?

If you are feeling particularly brave, ask your children (they can write it down and give it to you). "If you would change one thing about the way I parent, what would it be?" or, "Do you feel safe to tell me anything?"

Be willing to listen.

With me, the issues were pretty close to the surface; there was not very much digging to do. Most likely, this is the same for you. A very good way to see, who "owns" the problem, is to ask, "Is this MY problem?" (my kids want to express themselves in a way unique to them – piercings – hair colorings, etc. and I don't like it) or is it their problem (my child isn't getting good grades in school). We can support our kids with healthy boundaries and guidelines, give them honest feedback, offer to supply the necessary support or interventions (therapy, tutors, dietitians) but at some point we need to let them own their own problems. After all, they cannot solve it, nor learn to solve it, if they don't fully own it. Our baby birds are growing up and they are learning how to fly with their own wings and will often make miscalculated flights and/or crash landings. It would be optimal for them to do this when they are still young, land the consequences are not as detrimental as when they are older. We must allow them to learn this (and learn some things about ourselves in the process).

Am I willing to look at my child's behavior (and how they push my buttons) as a mirror to what is going on in me and *own* my stuff? Am I willing to do the work and heal the wounded parts of myself? Am I open to the possibility that my child just might be here to show me what those parts are?

When unkind or hurtful words or deeds come from me, I recognize that they are in me and it is time for me to stop the cycle of hurt. I can heal. I am worthy of healing. I love myself enough to give to myself that which I was deserving of as a child but did not receive. I silently bless my child for bringing this awareness to me. I think make amends with my child and tell them honestly about what I have just learned. Our children learn the most from us by watching what we do.

Something I have learned: My kids come through me – not to me. They are a reflection of themselves, their soul's lessons – not me. My job is to work myself out of a job.

Declaration: When I am nurturing and loving my children, I am nurturing and loving myself. What I give away to others, I embody in myself.

I Do Declare: _____

_____

_____

I am so grateful for: Unconditional Love – may we embody it, be it and give it away.

I am grateful for the great: _____

_____

_____

And the not so great: _____

_____

_____

I Jump for Joy when I ....

Raising my Exuberant level: In raising children, there are so many magical moments…and then there are those moments that can suck the energy out of you. Learning to check in with your energy and release the build-up can be highly effective. Stand tall and raise your arms to the sky (as if asking for serious help! ☺). Take in a deep cleansing breath, reaching down to the earth as if you were picking up the heaviest of loads. Now lifting your heavy load up to the heavens, and then with a great big exhale, release it, bending from the waist with a large exhalation breath! Then to ground yourself, take a stainless steel spoon and rub it over the bottom of your feet.

My Magical Moment: Buy sticky note pads (a different color for each member of your family). Randomly leave notes for your family…"I'm grateful to you for…" or "I really love how you," or "You are so special to me because…" The attitude of gratitude can turn mayhem into magic!

D.I.N.G. _____

_____

_____

CONSCIOUS KINDNESS

To thine own self be true... Was there something you did as a child that would really feel good? Find a way to let your wonder-child out to play. Buy and wear red lipstick!

Love thy neighbor... when you tuck your kids in tonight, tell them 5 things you REALLY love about them. Hold their hand, point to 1 thing per finger, then put a kiss in their hand, place it on their heart and tell them that the words and kisses stay with them forever! Or buy healthy suckers (found at the health store) and keep a few in your purse to offer a struggling mom with her kids in the store.

Never let it be said that to dream
is a waste of one's time.
For dreams are our realities in writing.
In dreams, we plant the seeds of our future.

Fun, Fun & More Fun Friday!

We know not where our dreams will take us,
but we can probably see quite clearly
where we'll go without them.
~ Marilyn Gray ~

Day 19

On Day 1 I had you fill in your intentions (your "really, really wants"). Go back and take a peek at those. What has your soul called you to do – even way back when you truly believed you could be anything or do anything. Remember *that* girl!? Yeah. She lives inside of you. She might be buried under a pile of "to do's" or obligatory expectations, but she remembers who you are and what your unique expression of the Divine came here to do. It's buried in your deepest longings.

In our attempts to be more efficient in our lives, we have backed ourselves into an all or nothing corner. I think sometimes we tell ourselves that if we can't do something all the way, we just don't do it at all. I recognize that thinking in myself. I finally named it. It's called fear. It surfaces as confusion because if I am *confused*, I don't have to examine my deep longings. I can simply whirl around all of the reasons why I am unable to explore them. Writing had called to me from the depth of my soul since I was a little girl. But the grown-up in me had a myriad of reasons why I would not be able to do this. Granted, most of them were valid from the reasonable mind. But as my soul's whisper became a louder roar, I realized there was another way. I simply needed to first recognize it, then give it a space to come forth and then step back and allow it.

Getting in touch with the unconscious part of ourselves (you know – the REAL driver of our car!) can be quite a fun expedition. One great project I had fun with was creating a Bagua Vision Board. Doing a vision board is a fabulous way to anchor your intentions with some eye-grabbing visuals.

A Bagua vision board is unique in that it is broken down into the 9 sectors of our lives, so we can get very specific about what we want to create in each of these areas. So, go grab some magazines, your favorite beverage, some great music and go digging! Cut out pictures or phrases that speak to you. Below is the model you'll be using. I used a medium sized poster board and added color to each of the squares. My board continued to evolve for several weeks. I found interesting (and unexpected) things calling to me. It is my hope that you find the same!

WEALTH	FAME	RELATIONSHIPS
Prosperity	Reputation	Love/Partnership
Gratitude	Integrity	Receptivity
Purple	**Red**	**Pink**
FAMILY	HEALTH	CREATIVITY
Community	Vitality	Children/Future
Group support	Balance	Joy
Green	**Yellow**	**White**
WISDOM	CAREER	HELPFUL
Self-improvement	Life Purpose	PEOPLE/TRAVEL
	Courage	Benevolence
Blue	**Black**	**Gray**

Something I have learned: I have come here for a purpose and I know my dreams and deep longings are great clues as to what that is! I can play around with my imagination and envision whatever I want to create!

Declaration: I am migrating toward that which I am vibrating…I am receiving what I am believing!

I Do Declare: _____

_____

_____

I am so grateful for: Blank pages and endless possibilities!

I am grateful for the great: _____

_____

_____

And the not so great: _____

_____

_____

I Jump for Joy when I ….

Raising my Exuberant level: Each day spend time with your vision board. Light a white candle and sit in front of it. See if you can recreate in your mind's eye the images. Pick a particular picture to focus on. Take a deep breath in and imagine breathing this intention all the way into your entire being. As you breathe out – anchor your intention in your breath and see it going out into the Universe. The cool thing about our breath, is that once it is out, it can no longer be traced back to us…it becomes one with the Universe. Hold that energy and awareness as you breathe your intention into the Universe!

My Magical Moment: Make your own Bagua Vision Board!

D.I.N.G. _____
_____
_____

CONSCIOUS KINDNESS

To thine own self be true…Find one small way to nurture something on your Bagua Vision board. If you want to travel, can you go to a travel agent and get a travel brochure? Little cracks.

Love thy neighbor…Do something for someone in secret….this is my favorite thing to do. Leave someone at the office a kind note and a chocolate – or send a teacher or principal an anonymous note about what a great job they are doing.

You are stronger than you feel-smarter than you think
and more beautiful than you could ever imagine!

Being kind isn't always easy or convenient.
But it has the potential to change everything.
~ Cap Watkins ~

Repeat after me: I am whole and perfect & so worthy of love!

***He who is plenteously
provided for from within,
needs but little from without.***

~ Johann Wolfgang Von Goethe ~

Me and My Shadow Saturday

*Not what we have
but what we enjoy,
constitutes our abundance.*
~ *John Petit-Senn* ~

Day 20

When my daughter was little, I would watch her engage in one of her favorite pastimes – pouring water. She was fascinated with pouring it from one container to another – over and over and over again. One time, she became frustrated because she was attempting to pour a large amount of water into a smaller container and it just wouldn't hold it. I watched and waited. She would get SO mad! However, eventually she figured out that if she used a larger container to pour the water into, it would work. I loved watching her process, without interfering and her own satisfaction at having achieved her goal.

How *big* is your container to receive? So often it seems we limit our capacity to receive because we just cannot contain it all. How much is enough, not enough or too much. Could you handle an endless, overflowing amount of good in *all* areas of your life?

This is true abundance. Receiving a compliment (with no explanation or rebuttal), and just saying thank you and taking it all the way in. Letting someone else volunteer to pick up the kids, do the laundry, bring the cupcakes for the school party, pick up the tab for lunch – without feeling guilty or a need to reciprocate. This is not to say that we don't give back. However, it we tend to talk about not having enough (be it sleep, money, time, energy), yet when we are offered more of each of these, are we able to accept it?

What does *true* abundance look like to you? Where do you feel like there is not enough for you? Can you gently examine how you feel about receiving more?

It's also interesting to look at how we hold onto that which we receive. Are we 'touching it lightly' or clinging to it with all our might? I have come to an understanding about that which I am *in possession of* versus the idea of *I possess*. This has made receiving an amazing process because it is a continual flow of coming AND going. I think it is what the saying "This too shall pass" really means. Having a capacity to receive is an amazing opportunity to truly be in the flow of life. When we recognize we are in possession of _____ (a job, house, relationship, children, etc.) instead of possessing them, the free flow of giving and receiving (including holding on and letting go) does not create so much angst for us.

In the Bible, it continually has the phrase, "And it came to pass..." A cursorily look at this would make it seem that this is an introductory statement. I believe that IT is the truth of a situation. All things are coming to pass. It becomes our lesson to get into the flow of them coming and going.

I have had an abundance of opportunities to let go of things I was trying to possess. In giving them up, I was able to receive so much more. Being open to receive also means we are open to be "in possession of" instead of possessing (as in not holding on so tight) and also be willing to let go.

What does being in the flow of my life look and feel like?

Then…

I know I really need to _____

_____

But I am scared because _____

_____

_____

Something I have learned: To be truly balanced, my capacity to receive must match my capacity to give. It's just like breathing – a constant and balanced flow of in and out.

Declaration: I am open to receive unending and bountiful abundance in all areas of my life. There is no limit to what I can have, be or do. I am opening my heart to receive.

I Do Declare: _____

_____

_____

I am so grateful for: unending abundance that comes to me now, under grace and in perfect order!

I am grateful for the great: _____

_____

_____

And the not so great: _____

_____

_____

I Jump for Joy when I ….

Raising my Exuberant level: Receiving energy can come from a myriad of ways. One very good way is to clear away things that clog our energy. Make a list of things that you can do where you feel a sense of mastery. This can look like: cleaning out the car, getting rid of the pile on the dining room table, answering emails, returning something to the store. These little "energy suckers" pile up and our thoughts about these things can keep us from receiving new energy. Make this your "Mastery" list. (It'll feel better than a "To Do Drudgery" List! Try to commit to checking off one a day (or even a week if you want!)

My Magical Moment: Decorate a bucket. Use permanent markers, stickers – or you can get really "Pinterest-y" and get a clay pot and decoupage pictures of what you are ready, willing and negotiating-being-able to receive. Leave it out and continually fill it up with words, pictures and representations of what you are wanting to receive. Buy some Lima beans and write with permanent marker what you are ready to receive. Then, plant them in your pot or bucket and see how they grow!

D.I.N.G. _____

_____

_____

CONSCIOUS KINDNESS

To thine own self be true... Write a love letter to yourself. Tell yourself all of the amazing and wonderful things about yourself that you truly love!

Love thy neighbor... Write a love letter to your spouse, partner or best friend...let them know how much they mean to you!

Thou has only to
follow the wall far enough
and there will be a door in it.
~ *Marguerite de Angeli* ~

Sacred Serenity Sunday

*Only in quiet waters things mirror themselves
undistorted. Only in a quiet mind is adequate
perception of the world.*
~ *Hans Margolius* ~

Day 21

Do you have a little place in your home you can call your own that is sacred? Is there a small corner of your bedroom, office or my favorite - the bathroom (You get a little bit of privacy there – unless you have kids under 5, then not so much! ☺) that you can create a sacred little spot?

I placed a small little cabinet in my bathroom and filled it with oracle cards, candles, sacred tokens, a journal and pen and random other things that were sacred to me. Later, I moved this space to my walk-in closet and now it is in the corner of my bedroom in my "sacred space" where I meditate each day. I could crawl into my little space and find some (if only momentarily) peace and quiet. I made a lot of decisions and found much comfort (and still do) in those sacred moments. But, I think it is the intention of having a space where you feel safe, at peace and anchored that allows you to open up. I think it is why we find peace in churches, synagogues or sacred dwelling places. The energy is anchored in openness. Our time is precious, so having a space to drop in and get quiet and let go makes it so much easier (and inviting) to do so.

I invite you today to think about creating such a space and filling it with some sacred things. Some ideas are: candles, sacred artifacts, journal, pen, incense, angels, a prayer shawl, sacred texts or books that inspire you, encouraging cards, or special stones. Minimally, place these items in a basket so that you have them accessible for when you want to drop in. Take time to bless the space with a special prayer.

Prayer has become for me, less asking and more attuning with the energy and vibration of love. Whenever I have anything that I am out of alignment with (or have been asked to pray for another person), I start by connecting with the energy of the person – trying to feel into the issue or condition of the person. Then I open myself up to unconditional love and "see" love flooding the problem or person. I know there is nothing that love cannot heal. In opening my heart up to love, I will either uncover a higher vibratory solution to the problem or I will be lifted into a more peaceful state about it as I await for the solution to reveal itself. I must resonate with the truth that if the problem is coming through me, than so must the solution. So, I must attune to the highest vibration I **can** in order to "lift up" the problem to a higher resolution. The Divine Sacred Energy of the Universe can only do as much through us as we are willing to allow. Our job is to open up to this flow and connect with it. Prayer then becomes more for me than the Divine. It is in this state that I can find out how to surrender and get more in the flow of the Divine Sacred Loving energy.

Something I have learned: When I open up to a little space for me, I can connect with the Divine Sacred Energy that is in and all around me.

Declaration: The essence of who I AM is whole and perfect and I am attuning myself in prayer to this truth.

I Do Declare: _____

_____

_____

I am so grateful for: quiet moments where I can connect to my highest self.

I am grateful for the great: _____

_____

_____

And the not so great: _____

_____

_____

I Jump for Joy when I ….

Raising my Exuberant level: A great way to raise one's vibration is to explore the relationship we have with the object of our desire. Spend some time reviewing your vision board and the "things" and states of beings you are intending to manifest. What is your energetic connection to those things *right* now? For example, if you wish to have more love in your life, what is your connection to love *right* now? Do you feel deserving? Does it seem to always elude you? Are you continually chasing it? If the law of attraction works that we attract what we ARE, not what we want, would want you are intending manifest? How can you find what you desire RIGHT now in your life, and more importantly within your own being? We are receiving at the level we are believing and behaving. Spend some time this week "being" what you want!

My Magical Moment: Collect, find or get sacred physical objects that are meaningful to you that represent that which you are intending to create. This can be a mirror, to see yourself more clearly, a candle if you want to bring in more light/clarity into your life, a plant for new life, pairs of little butterflies for new romance, a piggy bank for more money, a miniature car if you want to manifest a new car, etc. We create an intention and then we bring it into form. Little reminders of these "form" objects in our sacred space help us to focus on the physical connection of that which we wish to manifest.

D.I.N.G. _____
_____
_____

CONSCIOUS KINDNESS

To thine own self be true... What makes your soul giggle gleefully with joy? Find something that tickles your funny bone. Watch a comedy for 10-20 minutes. Laugh.

Love thy neighbor... Volunteer at your church or an organization that really speaks to you.

*How simple it is to see that
we can only be happy now,
and that there will never be a time
when it is NOT now.*

~ Gerald Jampolsky ~

Manifest It! Monday

*Freedom is that instant between when
someone tells you (or asks you) what to do and
when you decide how to respond.*
~ *Jeffrey Borenstein* ~

Day 22

When I first heard about the concept of mindfulness, my "mind" freaked out – thinking, "Yikes! Mind-FULL? That **is** the problem…my mind is full enough already – and mostly with useless stuff!" How is this gonna help!? However, as I began to practice this concept, I realized it is not necessarily all of the thoughts that cause the problems…it is my belief in them that creates my discomfort.

I began to view mindfulness as synonymous with being aware. I *liked* working with the concept of awareness. I found that my thoughts were going to come and go as they pleased – no amount of my struggling would change that. Just when I went "off duty", one would just sneak on in…like a teenager sneaking in after curfew! But, being aware of my thoughts…yeah. I could do that.

At the time I was learning this, I had a three-year-old who talked non-stop and was in constant need of attention and play, an almost sixteen year old in need of conversation, activity and oh, driving lessons (yikes!) and a fourteen-year old, who had recovered from autism, but still needed a lot of social opportunities, conversation **and** was home-schooling. Oh, all the while I was in school full-time, working full-time and was a

141

single Mommy and trying to fit in writing. My LIFE was a run-on sentence! I was living my life in pure oblivion and a lot of coffee. I could smell burnout coming over the coffee beans. I wanted, no needed to bring more awareness into my life. (Which seems like an oxymoron – why would I want to add one more thing to my oh-so-crazy-life?) Well, my comfort came in realizing that mindfulness/awareness was not about adding something, but by eliminating that which was unnecessary. From the unnecessary thoughts and chatter in my head, busy-work that kept me from feeling, to the toxic food, information and even people in my environment. As I became more aware of my feelings, I was able to process all of this with greater clarity.

So, I began a running commentary on what I was doing at the time (much to the great amusement of my children). For, I chose to do this by bringing the chatter on the inside – out.

I would say out loud, "I am taking my dishes to the sink." (I knew with the life I was living, I was going to need to make a concerted effort on this – so this is how I chose to do this!)

As you can imagine, my teens had a field day with this.

My daughter, "We are taking our mom to the mental institution." (Ah…kids are so precious!)

My son, "Mom, are you losing your mind?" (I think in his oh-so-black and white thinking, he might have had some fear of this!)

Me, "I sure hope so – or at least the incessant chatter in there…because it's not serving me so well!" I can play this game, too kids!

Blank stares. Then, laughter.

I may be crackin' up (or crackin' them up!), but from the cracks emerged a peacefulness and playfulness that had long been missing from my life and THAT they did see (and appreciated it, although it would be years before they told me so!)

First, I asked for the Universe's assistance and I asked Spirit/Love, my angels and guides to help me be aware. I asked, "Show me what I need to be aware of today. Let me be fully aware." I like to spell aware like this, **AWE – WHERE?** As in, in **awe** of **where** I am at right now. Can I practice the art of commitment in this moment to what is in front of me? No matter what that is.

Challenge for this week:

Be aware (in awe of where you are) in each moment. Even if you do not bring your internal commentary on the "outside" note where you are and what you are doing.

Something I have learned: No matter what I am doing, it is important and I put my full attention and heart into it. The Buddhists say, "Before enlightenment, chop wood, fetch water. After enlightenment, chop wood, fetch water." I believe the *enlightenment* is in the *knowing* you are there doing it.

Declaration: I am becoming clearer and present in each passing moment.

I Do Declare: _____

_____

_____

I am so grateful for: this moment.

I am grateful for the great: _____

_____

_____

And the not so great: _____

_____

_____

I Jump for Joy when I ….

Raising my Exuberant level: Choose one thing each day (brushing your teeth, eating, etc.) where you become completely and fully present and engaged. If you find yourself wandering, stop, take a breath and state 3 things that you see, hear, taste, smell, and feel in this moment. It'll ground you and bring you back to where you are.

My Magical Moment: Get clear and colored stones (you can usually find these at the Dollar Store). Get two glass containers (again, the Dollar Store has a wide selection). Each time you "catch" yourself being aware (as in "clear"), crop a clear stone in the first container. Whenever you "catch" yourself wandering, drop a colored stone. This is to measure and track your awareness. It's fun to see how much clearer and aware you can become, by, uh – being aware of it! Carry a clear stone in your purse as a reminder to be in awe of where you are!

D.I.N.G. _____

_____

_____

CONSCIOUS KINDNESS

To thine own self be true…Collect (or "Pin") special quotes that speak to you. When you have a few, print them and put them where you can see them (on your nightstand, in your bathroom, in your car).

Love thy neighbor…Print little positive quotes (I like to print them on business card stock) and when you leave a tip at a restaurant leave one behind.

When you own your own breath,
no one can steal your peace.
~ Author Unknown ~

Treat Me Right Tuesday

Inhale, and God approaches you.
Hold the inhalation, and God remains with you.
Exhale, and you approach God.
Hold the exhalation, and surrender to God.
~ Krishnamacharya ~

Day 23

We have looked at what it is we want to change (little cracks to allow a little "light" into our darkened corners). How is that going for you? Have you found some things more difficult than others? Wherever you are at – remind yourself in this moment, you are exactly where you need to be. Breathe. A compass, even moved by one degree will eventually land you in an entirely new place. So, keep moving forward. Just the "thought" of making a change is making a change!

One of my favorite quotes is, "Remember, life is not made up of the number of breaths we take, but by the moments that take our breath away." But, I have to be honest, there have been breathless moments and those have come because I have had the wind knocked out of me! You know those moments I'm talking about. Today, we're going to focus on our breath. Are you holding your breath right now? Where are you breathing from? Do you fill your lungs all the way down into your belly? Our breath is our life force and a lot of times it is getting sucked right out of us.

We want to take a few moments each day to practice deep, cleansing, relaxing and restorative breathing. Andrew Weil has created a breath that he uses with a lot of his clients for anti-anxiety. I like to combine this breath (what can I say, I like to get the "most" out of my moments, as I have found with a busy household, full-time job, and when I was in school full-time, I wanted to make the most of my moments!) with a few other things. The first is a heart-centered thought. The second is visualizing white light streaming in with the in-breath and dark cloudy toxic yuckiness (do you have a good visual now?) coming out with the out-breath.

Start with a heart-centered thought. Now if you are having a particularly difficult time with someone, try visualizing something you love about him or her. It will help open up your heart chakra. With my kids, I try to keep a "go to" memory – something that always melts my heart…my daughter with her Dorothy Glitter-Red slippers on the wrong feet do it for me every time! You get the idea…something that makes you smile and warms you from the inside out.

Then you take an in-breath (visualizing white light streaming in through your nose – or the crown of your head) for the count of 4.

Then you hold it for the count of 7 (while visualizing this white, healing light filling every cell of your body).

Then you breathe out all of the toxic thoughts, feelings, beliefs, anger, frustration, blah-blah-blah that is sitting inside of your mind, body, and spirit to the count of 8.

You repeat this until you feel "clear" energy coming out.

Something I have learned: No one can breathe for me. I must do this myself. I want to stop holding my breath (literally and figuratively).

Declaration: My breath connects me to my highest Self. When I take a breath, I am breathing in the divine light and wisdom of the entire Universe and am breathing out all negatively. I am breathing with ease. (Or I am learning to breathe with ease - ☺).

I Do Declare: _____

_____

_____

I am so grateful for: the life energy that flows through you and me and connects us.

I am grateful for the great: _____

_____

_____

And the not so great: _____

_____

_____

I Jump for Joy when I ….

Raising my Exuberant level: There is a great breathing technique for grounding and balancing called Square breathing. With this, you inhale for the count of 4. You hold for a count of 4. You blow out for a count of 4. Then, you just pause (neither inhaling nor exhaling) for the count of 4. To ensure you are breathing deep into your belly, lay down and place a small bean bag or pillow on top of your stomach so that you can see it going up and down with your breath.

My Magical Moment: Isn't it nice that we are being breathed? (Especially in those moments when we are not *consciously* practicing our breathing – like sleeping!) For a magical, peaceful and rejuvenating sleep, make an affirmation pillowcase. This is a great activity for the entire family. Buy white pillowcases. Get fabric markers and write calming, loving words and affirmations on them. You can even ask other people (your family, friends) to add their "love" to your pillowcase. As you fall asleep you can breathe in deeply these beautiful loving words.

D.I.N.G. _____

_____

_____

CONSCIOUS KINDNESS

To thine own self be true... Give yourself a sensory meditation. Buy a favorite treat, find a lovely spot outside and sit down, savor every morsel of your treat and let it fill you all the way up. Feel the sensory pleasure of honoring your taste buds!

Love thy neighbor... Bake cookies or some "homemade" goods for your neighbor!

Be thankful for what you have;
You'll end up having more.
Think about what you don't have,
you will never have enough.
~ Oprah Winfrey ~

How I Wonder & Wander Wednesday

Before the truth can set you free,
you have to discover what lie
is holding you hostage.
~ Rachel Wolchin ~

Day 24

I wonder what our lives would look like if we opened up to what we really, really wanted? Take a moment right now and *feel* this desire and from here we will set clear, concise intentions.

Let's look at our deep longings. What have we <u>always</u> wanted to do? Then order them based on how much we have wanted to do them.

1.
2.
3.
4.
5.
6.
7.
8.
9.
10.

Now, let's look at the *relationship* we have with what we desire.

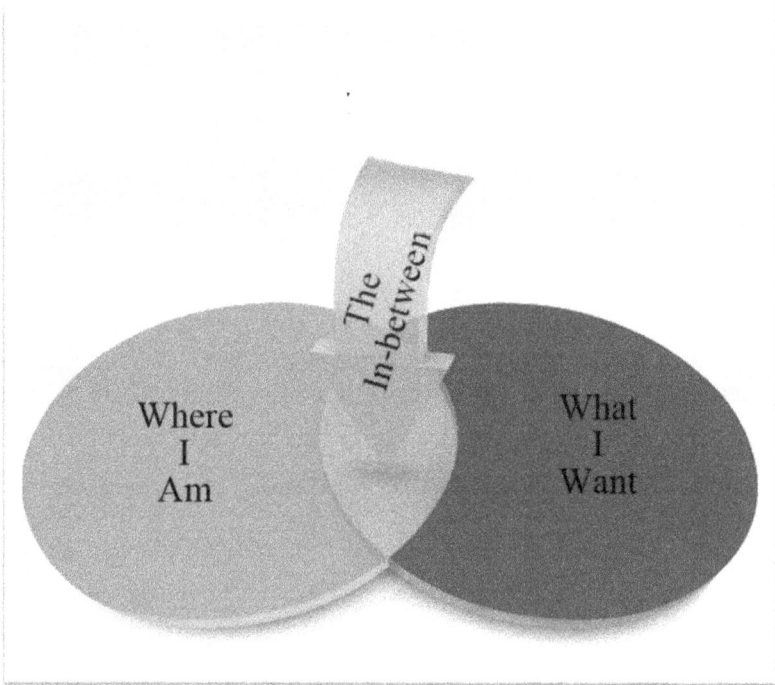

Can you find a relationship between you and that which you desire? For example, if you have a desire for a new job, place in the right bubble new job and the qualities of that job. Place in the left bubble the qualities that you possess and would like to utilize at this new job. Find the ways in which you already vibrate with the new job you want.

Now ask yourself, what does the job *represent*? (Is it freedom – either financially or with your time, or is it security, or flexibility? What is it you are *truly* seeking from the job?) Now, go back and look at where you are. If you ultimately want more freedom, where (or how) in your life are you NOT experiencing freedom? The in-between space is the relationship between where you are and what you want.

<u>You must BECOME that which you want.</u>

Huh? Yes, you heard me.

When something is outside of us, it is perceived as "missing". To bring in more freedom, we must become it. Like attracts like.

To do this, we discover what we ultimately want (which usually is different then what we are *thinking* we want), and then find ways to integrate this underlying feeling (freedom, flexibility, love, security, etc.).

As we are crackin' up and letting in light, we want to first look at our desires and then look just underneath them. That is where the real truth lies. Here's an example, Mary Jane El Borolife goes out one night. She is immediately intrigued by the lead guitarist on stage and during his breaks the two of them share a few drinks, a great conversation, and ultimately phone numbers. Mary Jane has attracted LG (lead guitarist) because she is open and receptive. However, while awaiting his call she becomes less *receptive* and more *pursuant* as she is very much wanting LG to call her – doing her affirmations, lighting up her candles and visualizing their impending marriage! Upon further investigation, Mary Jane El Borolife recognizes that LG represents fun, excitement and a lifestyle much different from her current life. As she focuses on bringing more fun and excitement into her own life (becoming what she wants), she is less pursuant to LG. Whether LG calls or not becomes irrelevant, as he might not have been that great for her after all – just merely awakening the slumbering part of her! She has no control over whether he calls her or not. But, as she realizes he is merely there to remind her of a part of herself she is not nurturing, she *becomes* the fun, adventurous energy she is seeking. (Most likely if she is still desirous of a relationship, she will now attract that which she is now vibrating at!)

If you are feeling stifled, how can you integrate a little more freedom? It might not be in your job (right now), but is there a way to integrate the *feeling* of freedom where you are right now?

Nelson Mandela said this, "It is always impossible until it is done." He used his experience as fuel and burnt it up to propel him on toward such amazing things! His imprisonment could have been "the end" for him. From the great work he accomplished after his release, it is clear his imprisonment was a beginning! He is only one of many great examples of individuals who use their experience to live out their life purposes.

This is ultimately how we're going to get where we want to go. We have to start where we are at. We have to use what we have (what we are experiencing and where we are at in this current moment) as fuel by learning to digest it (take out what we need, and get rid of the rest) and connect to the *feeling* of what we want. This feeling goes out as energy to the Universe. When we are *feeling* in "formlessness" (energy) free or abundant, loved, cherished, happy, healthy, prosperous, we attract the same in form (matter).

You have probably heard the saying, "you are receiving what you are believing." I would like to add to this.

You migrate toward that which you vibrate!

The definition of migrate is "to move from one part of something toward another." When you are *feeling* into what you want, you are connecting to that which you are moving toward.

Find what your relationship is to that which you want. As in, what is just below the surface of what you truly desire. Then connect to that feeling. Then spend some time (according to research about 16 seconds is all it takes!) anchoring the *feeling-a-zation* (it's like a visualization with feeling!) of what you really, really want! This will involve all of your senses. Can you *see* yourself in the visualization (using our example, see yourself at your new job – what are you wearing? What do you smell, taste, feel, hear? Do you see yourself smiling, laughing, "hi-fiving" your co-workers as you *feel* the experience of that which you wish to manifest?)

Try this for several days. Then turn your "want" into an intention. Instead of, "I want to secure a great-paying job/position where I am using my gifts and talents and being abundantly compensated for all that I give and do!" Change that to "I intend to…" Anchor that with another *feeling-a-zation* of having already achieved this. Does it feel different? Are you doing a little fist-pumping, woo-hooing and celebratory dinners with your friends?

Now we're going to really amp it up with gratitude. When we can look at where we are at, we can create a bridge using gratitude to infuse the situation with light to carry us to where we want to go.

What we end up doing is taking that which we have been rejecting and do not want in our lives (treating it like poison we wish to spit out) and using it as fuel to "burn" to propel us toward what we want. Our "wants" serve as keys to open the doors to our hearts truest desires.

Something I have learned: My heart's truest desires lie just beneath the surface of what I want!

Declaration: I am opening my heart wide to my desires!

I Do Declare: _____

_____

_____

I am so grateful for: my yummy, juicy desires! They point me to what is mine to do!

I am grateful for the great: _____

_____

_____

And the not so great: _____

_____

_____

I Jump for Joy when I ….

Raising my Exuberant level: While tapping between your eyebrows with your index finger, in the morning when you arise, give thanks (in advance) for that which you wish to create this day. At the end of the day, while tapping between your eyebrows with your index finger, give thanks for 5 things!

My Magical Moment: Buy a neon poster and hang it somewhere you can see it. Add gratitudes each day. Get a small coupon-sized expandable file. Create "files" of areas in your life (from your Bagua board). Whenever you see signs of these things coming into fruition, write it down and file it away.

D.I.N.G. _____

_____

_____

CONSCIOUS KINDNESS

To thine own self be true... What is something you used to do for yourself that you no longer do? Find a way to fit it into your life. Even if you have to make a variation (used to get pedicures, but your budget is a little tighter – buy a new nail polish and "treat" yourself to candles, aromatherapy, a chocolate and new nail polish!)

Love thy neighbor... Tell a perfect stranger something kind that you noticed about them!

One of the happiest moments in life
is when you finally have the courage
to let go of
what you cannot change.

We're in This Together Thursday

I'm letting you go.
You let me go a long time ago.
I realize, it is time for me to do the same.

Day 25

What (or who) are you holding onto that is no longer holding onto you? Is there a belief, a circumstance, a projection, un-forgiveness, hope, idealized situation or person that you just need to release? Many times we hold onto anger because we feel like we don't want to let the other person off the hook. But in so doing, we continue hurting ourselves by holding onto them or what they did.

It is my belief that everything is energy and we are connected to all things. Doesn't holding on to the anger connect us energetically to the very person we wish to be free of? It would seem (as anger tends to have such intensity) that the *hold* would be even stronger through anger. Why do we do it? Anger can be a very good thing - as it is often the fuel we need to make necessary changes in our lives. It's like the little fire-starters we use to light a candle or a fire. However, once the candle or fire is lit, we don't need to continue feeding it. It can also serve to protect us and move us toward action in a particular area of our lives that needs attention. It serves a purpose, but as we crack open to let in a little more light, we want to examine if we're holding onto anger that needs to be let go of.

161

To me, letting go and forgiveness can be the greatest gift I ever give myself. When I choose to forgive it is because I wish to **give** up anger, frustration, sad, hopelessness, hurt **for** peace, love, harmony, joy. It is an exchange and one in which I benefit so much from.

David Hawkins says in his book *Letting Go*, that there is a scientific basis when Jesus tells us to bless and love our enemies. Anger and hate vibrate at a lower level of energy, whereas, forgiveness vibrates at a higher level of energy. When we shift our lower energy (anger, hate, etc.) to a higher vibration of forgiveness we create a psychic shield on an energetic level and are not psychically vulnerable to the other person. That seems like a pretty good reason to give forgiveness a go, wouldn't you say?

What if it is myself I need to forgive? Yeah. That one, although seemingly obvious, can be the most difficult. We tend to be our own worst enemies sometimes. So, what can we do? We can first of all, make restitution (if possible) for what we have done, or say I'm sorry, or tell a friend or confidant in order to release it. We can also recognize that "good judgment comes from experience and experience comes from bad judgment." Sometimes we have to learn lessons through a not-so-conventional way. Some of my lessons have been learned in the calm and some (ok, most) have been learned in the storm.

What or who do you need to let go of to lighten your load? Who could you let off the hook (including yourself) that is piercing your *own* life?

You can write a goodbye letter. Put it in an envelope. Seal it. Burn it (yeah…I'm a big fan of fire!). Then gather the ashes. Put them "on ice" (in an ice cube tray with water). Freeze them. Then, use the ice cubes on your plants. Let Mother Nature take the old and recycle it into the new.

Something I have learned: When I am able to let go of the good, I can make way for the great in my life. I can release into love all (including people) that no longer serves a purpose in my life.

Declaration: I am releasing and letting go. I am (open to becoming) whole, healed and loved.

I Do Declare: _____

_____

_____

I am so grateful for: the ability to choose to let go of what no longer serves me.

I am grateful for the great: _____

_____

_____

And the not so great: _____

_____

_____

I Jump for Joy when I ….

Raising my Exuberant level: Pick up all of the heaviness in your mind, body and spirit as if you were picking up a huge boulder from the earth. Then with a GREAT BIG SIGH, bending from the waist, releasing it to Mother Earth to heal and recycle. Then, with your Hands up into the sky bringing heaven and Divine Love into your heart, feel your heart filling up with love.

My Magical Moment: Get one black and one white candle – any size but a candle you can write on. You will write on the black candle all that you would like to release. Pick a time when you can write or journal about this release so that you can be very clear who, and what you are releasing. Write it on the black candle and light it up and burn it down. You can choose to do this in small increments or all at once. Once the black candle is completely burned up, light a white candle. This candle represents the Divine opening up a space to clear away the old and energetically shift the lower vibration of unforgiveness to the higher vibration of love. If you feel inclined you can write on the white candle, "I forgive……(name or situation) and invite love in to clear this energy."

D.I.N.G. _____

_____

_____

CONSCIOUS KINDNESS

To thine own self be true…Get rid of that one pair of jeans that mock you – you know the ones I'm talking about…"When I lose the extra 1-pounds, I'll be able to get into these!" Toss 'em and go get yourself a new pair of jeans! Release any judgment!

Love thy neighbor…Offer to bring your child's teacher lunch (or a co-worker or friend).

The reluctance to put away childish things
may be a requirement of genius.
~ Rebecca Pepper Sinkler ~

Fun, Fun & More Fun Friday!

Chaos should be regarded as
extremely good news.
~ *ChogyamTrungpa* ~

Day 26

Ah…chaos. Chaos is defined as "the science of surprises, teaching us to expect the unexpected." One of the principles of the Chaos Theory is called The Butterfly Effect. In a nutshell, it is the power to cause a hurricane in China, simply by a butterfly flapping its wings in New Mexico. Now, it may take a very long time for this to happen – but the connection is real! In other words, small changes can lead to drastic results over time! Isn't this exciting?

In exploring the principles of chaos, we would like to try to integrate these principles into our lives (life is chaotic and when we can view this not only as a good thing and the way it is we can also see that it is actually here to move us along!) It is unpredictable. We never know what might happen during chaos – there are endless possibilities. Despite what it looks like, there is an order!

So, how can we "flap our wings", if ever-so-lightly? Well, we're going to have to set an intention. Out of the chaos we an open up to the endless possibilities that are available to us.

We have been integrating, affirming, breathing, and becoming more aware. How are you feeling? Are you loving yourself through this?

167

Are you being compassionate with yourself? Sometimes, our tendency is to look at where we are failing and not measuring up. Let's drop the "report card" mentality for a moment and honor our progress thus far. Let us honor our commitment to change for the better. Stop. Breathe in all of the love from the Universe. *Can you feel me sending you a hug* ☺*?* As you take in a deep breathe, feel the love coming through this book, as Spirit is flowing through me, into these words directly to you. Breathe it all in. You are a beautiful butterfly changing the world by changing you! Wow. How powerful is that!? YOU are so worth every second of this *time* you are taking for yourself.

Which leads us to our last area of health-related integrated wellness. Time. Stop your screaming, girl! I *know* you don't have enough of it as it is, huh? We will work on that skewed thought-perception with our affirmations this week. Once we *intend* to make an improvement, demonstrate our faith in the Universe to support us, voilà – the rest is pure magic! Are you with me? Ready for a little wing-flapping?

Choose one of the following (or substitute your own) and intend to "date" yourself once this week. My hope is that this will become a *must* in your life ☺. I found myself so much more available for others when I started taking this time for myself. If it scares you, be with that…with compassion and non-judgment. Sometimes it is difficult to get what we need because 1) we don't even know what that looks like as it is has been such a long time since we have even entertained the notion that we have needs and, 2) it's hard to ask. Even from ourselves.

First, I will give you some ideas (which will most likely stimulate ideas of your own). Secondly, you will make the time. Even if you need to "date" yourself at home, put the kids to bed early and carve out time for you. We must make this a priority. When something becomes important to us – *really* important to us – we find a *way*, if not, we'll find a reason not to. Let us find a *way*, shall we?

- Take yourself to a picnic (buy the food YOU want and treat yourself to something delicious.) Squeeze in an extra ½ hour before picking the kids up for a "treat" just for you! (Hide the wrappers…they children will find your evidence! ☺)
- Take a long hot bath with bubbles (or my favorite detox bath with 1 C. Sea Salt, 1 C baking soda and a few drops of lavender and scoop of coconut oil…feels good and detoxes too!)
- Take a hike to a new place.
- Buy a magazine you love and find a cozy spot to read it.
- Buy a coloring book and fabulous gel pens or markers.
- Rent a chick flick to watch when no one is around.
- Buy an exotic fruit and eat it mindfully.
- Buy a flower for yourself.
- Get a decadent chocolate for yourself.
- Go to the park and swing.
- Get a pedicure.
- Go to the museum.
- Browse a bookstore.
- Get a massage.
- Go to the movies (alone!)
- Go out to a restaurant – by yourself – all dressed up.
- Go to a concert or Broadway show by yourself.
- Buy a spa treatment – make a plan for the day.

- Take a pottery class.
- Buy canvases at a craft store and paint.
- Go to the community center and see if they have a class that interests you.
- Learn how to belly dance.

We are just playing with the idea of investing in ourselves. There are so many ways to do this – all of them unique to YOU, but as we explore ourselves, our needs and desires, the ideas will just pour in. We're just crackin' the door open a little!

Something I have learned: I am worth making time for and as I learn to love myself more and more, I enjoy the company I keep when alone!

Declaration: There is always enough time and the Universe supports me in all ways. I am always on Divine time. I am creating time to nurture myself.

I Do Declare: _____
_____
_____

I am so grateful for: time...there is always just the right amount.

I am grateful for the great: _____
_____
_____

And the not so great: _____

_____

_____

I Jump for Joy when I ….

Raising my Exuberant level: Check out the Chinese Organ clock. It shows particular organs associated with times. Do you awaken at the same time each night? Or are you sluggish at the same time every day? Find out when your energy is depleted and see if you can find ways to support that particular organ in a healthy way.

Time of Day	Organ	Associated with
11:00 p.m. – 1:00 A.M.	GALLBLADDER	Gallstones – Sleep & regenerate! Subconscious feelings of resentment may appear at this time. Emotion: Anger
1:00 A.M. – 3:00 A.M.	LIVER	Alcohol, chemicals, poor diet, need to detox liver. Deep resting & dreaming! Emotion: Anger, frustration & rage.
3:00 A.M. – 5:00 A.M.	LUNGS	Expelling toxins from the lungs. Sleep soundly! Emotion: Grief
5:00 A.M. – 7:00 A.M.	LARGE INTESTINES	Wake up & drink water! Emotions of defensiveness or feelings of being stuck could be evoked during this time. Emotion: Grief
7:00 A.M. – 9:00 A.M.	STOMACH	Digestion at its best. Eat breakfast! Emotions of disgust or despair likely to be stirred at this time. Emotion: Worry
9:00 A.M. – 11:00 A.M.	SPLEEN/ PANCREAS	Mental powers and converting nutrients into energy. Work & be active! Emotions of low self-esteem can be stirred at this time. Emotion: Worry
11:00 A.M. – 1:00 P.M.	HEART	Eat lunch & socialize! Emotions of extreme joy or sadness can be invoked at this time. Emotion: Joy

Time of Day	Organ	Associated with
1:00 P.M. – 3:00 P.M.	SMALL INTESTINE	The body is digesting lunch. Solve you problems & get organized! Vulnerable thoughts or feelings of abandonment may emerge. Emotion: Joy
3:00 P.M. – 5:00 P.M.	BLADDER	Best time for efficient work. Work, study & drink water! Feeling timid or irritated may occur now. Emotion: Fear
5:00 P.M. – 7:00 P.M.	KIDNEYS	Kidneys store energy. If tired, where did you spend your energy? Eat dinner & restore your energy. Emotion: Fear
7:00 P.M. – 9:00 P.M.	PERICADIUM	This is responsible for circulation, brain and reproductive organs. Socialize, flirt & have fun! Difficulty expressing emotions may occur during this time. Emotion: Joy
9:00 P.M. – 11:00 P.M.	TRIPLE WARMER	Thyroid, adrenals – responsible for energy, temperature & metabolism. Chill out, relax & read! Feelings of paranoia or confusion may occur during this time. Emotion: Joy

My Magical Moment: Take a beautiful piece of stationary or colored paper. Write all of your wing-flapping intentions on it (all of the ways in which you are going to love and nurture yourself). Now accordion fold it (folding ½ inch, and then turn it over, folding another ½ inch until the entire paper looks like an accordion). Now gather it in the middle (using ribbon, a pipe-cleaner, or clothespin). Put your beautiful "intention" butterfly somewhere where you are reminded to flap your wings!

D.I.N.G. _____

_____

_____

CONSCIOUS KINDNESS

To thine own self be true...(OK, I'll admit this is a silly one – but one I found myself continually *not* doing). Are you stopping regularly to honor your bladder? Are you drinking enough water so that you *have* to go enough throughout the day? It matters. It is a small, yet significant way to honor thy self! ☺

Love thy neighbor... Give your kid a "fun break" day and take them to do something fun. Or surprise them with lunch at school!

And the day came when the risk to remain tight in a bud
was more painful
than the risk it took to blossom.

~ Anais Nin ~

One day a student went to his Teacher for help.
"What am I doing wrong, Master? I plant seeds
in my garden, but they never come up."
"Tell me what you are doing," said the Teacher.
"Well, every day I plant and water. Then, at night,
I go to sleep, but in the middle of the night,
I wake up and get worried that the seeds
might not be growing.
So I go outside, dig them up and sure enough,
they are not growing!"
"I think I understand your problem,"
Said the Teacher.
~ Saaid Shakur Chrishti (Neil Douglas-Klotx) ~
April 2004

175

Me and My Shadow Saturday

Leap – and the net will appear!
~ Zen saying ~

Day 27

We have hopefully shed some light into the darkened corners of our minds, bodies and spirits over the last few weeks. It is analogous to planning seeds – but just like the story on the previous page, we have to allow the seeds to germinate and grow (with some nurturing along the way, too!)

If we have adjusted our compasses even ever-so-slightly, we have already plotted a new course. Now, we just must continue along our path and allow time to get where we are going.

The greatest gift we can give ourselves along this path is our unconditional love – all the time – no exceptions! We start with kindness – to all things, all the time (yes, that means to ourselves!) We all stumble, get up and move on, stumble and get up and move on. It is a continual process. How we learn to nurture ourselves and treat ourselves when we have fallen is a lesson in grace. It is amazingly simple. It is just not easy. Once we have learned to give this gift to ourselves, it is surprising how easily it pours of us onto others.

I hope our time together has given you a more gentle, loving and kind way of being with yourself. I hope there are no more punishing or harsh words being spoken to yourself by yourself (and if they do arise, may the crackin' up-and-into-more-light part of yourself rush in to self-correct!) May you see yourself as I do – whole, perfect and in need of no "fixing" – merely loved back into place.

We have one last "project" together. We worked on letting go of things or people that no longer served us on Thursday. Today, we will pack up for a little hike – down into the recesses of our selves. I will be there with you, holding your hand.

I would like you to picture yourself at a young age. Whatever age pops into your mind is the right age. I would like you to see you and your younger self sitting outside – perhaps under a tree, maybe on a mountain top or maybe you had a secret place you liked to go to when you were little. Go there now.

I just want you to ask her. What does she need from you? Listen. Journal if you'd like. Then ask her what you need to let go of to be free? Are there parts of yourself that have been unloved, punished and shoved into a deep, dark cave? Invite them out into the light. Remind her that you are safe. If you need the security of another person, do this with a friend, counselor, or someone who can lovingly hold this space for you. As you look around, imagine that each thing you need to release is now in the physical form of a rock. Notice its shape, size, texture, color.

Now, picture in your mind a very colorful backpack appearing. You and your little girl will go pick up the backpack. You and she will together pick up the rocks you see that represent the physical form of that which you are going to release and place them into the backpack. You place the backpack on your back (you are so much stronger than you have ever imagined yourself to be!) You hold your little girl's hand. Feel the energy of Love surrounding you, supporting you and assisting you as you go.

Now, we begin our climb. We will climb to the highest mountain. The backpack is heavy and weighing you down, but you are able to crawl up the last few steps. As you fall down from the weight of the backpack, it falls to the ground. Now, taking each rock – one at a time and kneeling holding each one in both of your hands and the hands of your little girl, see the ray of the Divine light of love shining down upon it and transforming it into a dove. It belongs to Divine Love. Send it on its way. See it fly to the sun. After you have released all of your rocks to Divine Light & Love, you see that your backpack has transformed into a parachute. You put it on, with your little girl on your back and leap into the air. You are flying now!

You have so *earned your wings!!!*

> ***When you come to the edge***
> ***of all the light you have,***
> ***and must take a step***
> ***into the darkness of the unknown,***
> ***either there will be***
> ***something solid to stand on….***
> ***or you will FLY!!!***

Something I have learned: Crackin' up has allowed me to excavate more light than I ever imagined possible! I can no longer be afraid of the sea for I have learned to sail my own ship!

Declaration: I am continually learning to love myself deeper and fuller, nurture myself and play each and every day!

I Do Declare: _____

_____

_____

I am so grateful for: you and the courage you have!

I am grateful for the great: _____

_____

_____

And the not so great: _____

_____

_____

I Jump for Joy when I ….

Raising my Exuberant level: Get some magnets (I found some at the Dollar Store!) and while saying that which you wish to release, holding them in your right hand, stand up and move them up your chakras (about

2 inches from your body). Do this at least seven times or as many as you feel to clear this. Then, put the magnets in your left hand, and using an anchoring statement (either an affirmation of what you want, or a simple, "I am healed. I am loved. I am open to receive." Then raising the magnets above your head (pulling energy from up above), bring it in through your crown chakra and all the way down. Repeat at least seven times, or as many as you feel necessary.

My Magical Moment: Write what you wish to release about yourself (beliefs, thoughts, punishing ways) on rocks then throw them into a lake, river or stream or out into the desert.

If it is a person, cut out a paper heart. Write your name and the name of the other person on the heart. While ripping it apart, say -

"The conflict on this paper heart, is now released and pulled apart." Then, while putting it back together with "healing salve" (tape) say, "For I know only love is real, for you_____ (person's name) Divine Love is all I now feel."

D.I.N.G. _____

_____

_____

You are stronger than you feel-smarter than you think
and more beautiful than you could ever imagine!

CONSCIOUS KINDNESS

To thine own self be true... Visit a health store and look around at some alternative snacks, lotions, deodorants, toothpastes without chemicals. Just a small crack to care for our Goddess bodies!

Love thy neighbor... Get $10.00 in $1's and drop them randomly throughout the day (or two $5's)...how fun for the lucky recipient to find money lying around! ☺

The Prayer of Saint Francis

O Lord, make me an instrument of Thy Peace!
Where there I hatred, let me sow love;
Where there is injury, pardon;
Where there is discord, harmony;
Where there is doubt, faith;
Where there is despair, hope
Where there is darkness, light, and
Where there is sorrow, joy.
Oh Divine Master, grant that I may not
So much seek to be consoled
As to console;
To be understood as to understand,
To be loved as to love;
For it is in giving that we receive;
It is in pardoning, that we are pardoned;
And it is in dying that we are born to Eternal Life.

Sacred Serenity Sunday

Prayer is not asking.
Prayer is putting yourself in the hands of the Divine,
at The Divine's disposition,
and listening to the voice
in the depths of our hearts.
~ Mother Theresa ~

Day 28

Wow…here we are – twenty-eight days later! How are you feeling? It is my greatest intention and prayer that you are feeling more whole – with a little more light infused into the darkened corners of your life. I see you resonating with Divine light and energy that radiates Love and Truth.

I began this book with a partial prayer by St. Francis of Assisi. I end with its entirety. It is a prayer I say with my whole heart each day. I love the visual of being an instrument of peace.

What kind of instrument are you? For we are a beautiful orchestra that plays the Divine Music of life and love through us. We are each unique and necessary for the music to be harmonious and beautiful.

As the energy of the Universe flows through me, music is made. My work is in keeping the space open, so that nothing is impeding the flow of air! ☺ As we have looked into shedding light into the areas of darkness, they are all in an attempt to unclog our instrument.

I like to think of myself as a flute…and there are so many different kinds of flutes…whether it is a hand-carved Native America piece of art, or alto flute, or soprano flute, each one of our instruments is uniquely designed to serve our highest purpose. However, the essence of what is inside is the same – a clear pathway for air (The Divine) to pass through.

One way that I have learned to keep my pathway clear is meditation, the other most powerful way, is through prayer. Now I have negotiated my relationship with prayer since I was a little girl in a Baptist church where prayer looked like either begging forgiveness from a very angry, disappointed Daddy-God, to a Genie-in-a-bottle-wish-grantor-if-I-was-good-God. Crack. As a little light came into my life, I pondered maybe that prayer was more for me than the Divine. The Divine, was already *there*, prayer was my work to get me in alignment with the Truth, which was that everything was **already** in Divine Order. My job was to first, do what I could (The Divine can do no more for me than through me) secondly, accept things the way they were, third, release my need for them to be different and lastly, open my heart to the promptings of what **I** could do regarding what it was I was praying about.

Prayer began to look like this for me: I would first quiet my mind through meditation and then connect with the energy of the person or thing I was intending to pray about. After feeling the connection, I would see myself floating up. As I would continue to open my heart, generally tears would begin to roll spontaneously down my face. I would feel a Presence flowing through me. There were never any words necessarily accept for a silent (and sometimes audible) thank you. Then, I would release it (or in particular, my attachment to the outcome). The greatest gift from this time was the overwhelming sense of peace and grace that would flood my entire being.

As you are crackin' open and letting in more light and clearing the pathways for the Divine to flow through, may you feel lighter, a greater sense of peace, and Divine love flowing in, through and as you. May the Grace of the Divine kiss you gently on the forehead each and every day!

Something I have learned: When I pray, it is my soul tuning into and *up* to the Divine.

Declaration: I am a divine, clear instrument through which love flows.

I Do Declare: _____

_____

_____

I am so grateful for: our connection – in and through love!

I am grateful for the great: _____

_____

_____

And the not so great: _____

_____

_____

I Jump for Joy when I ….

Raising my Exuberant level: Make an "I can choose peace rather than this" can. Get a mason jar, and cover it with white paper. Write the words "I can choose peace rather than this" on the paper. Decorate it with words about peace/feeling safe, etc. Whenever you have a worry enter into your consciousness, write it down and "can it." Stick it in here with the lid on. Make a commitment to let it go and not look at it again. Each Sunday, take out your worries and review them. How many of them *actually* even happened? The ones that you need to do something about do so. The other ones, leave on your alter and allow the Divine to take them.

My Magical Moment: Open up your "My new 28-Day-Later Self" letter. How are you feeling?

D.I.N.G. _____
_____
_____

CONSCIOUS KINDNESS

To thine own self be true... Do something scrumptious for yourself – you so deserve to celebrate your journey today! I am joining your celebration in spirit...a toast – to you!!

Love thy neighbor... Choose someone in your life to encourage, pray for and send loving thoughts and light to for the next 30 days!

Difficult things take a long time,
impossible things a little longer.
~Author Unknown ~

My hope is that you have cracked open some space in your life to let light in. I know I've been crackin' up for years – and I have never felt so whole!

We have merely scratched the surface in our attempts to crack up! We've looked at areas in our lives that need a little light.

We began this road trip with some music, so I'll end on this note (yes, pun intended!) *My Wish* by Rascal Flatts.

Although we may never meet in person, I know we have "met" along this path. I see you. You are stronger than you feel, smarter than you think and more beautiful than you can ever imagine! I love you! *Lisa*

If we are facing in the right direction,
all we have to do is keep on walking.
~Buddhist Saying ~

Dear Self,

This is going to be YOUR year.
So dust off your sh*t kickers
And let's get started!

Love, Me

The world is full of people
who will go their whole lives
and not actually LIVE one day.

~

She did not intend
on being one of them!

You go, girl! ☺

ABOUT THE AUTHOR

Lisa Smith was born and raised in Ohio but moved to Phoenix, AZ twenty-five years ago where she currently resides with 2 of her 5 children (ages 11 – 28).   Lisa's son was diagnosed with autism at age 3 ½. This began an "off the beaten path" journey for Lisa which has led her down many interesting, adventurous and sometimes scarcely lit roads! However, the lessons in love learned along the way have been worth every twist and turn. Oh, and one of these *twists* led her to all she needed to aide in the healing of her son's autism. He is now 22 and considered autistic-free!   Lisa has a master's degree in Child and Adolescent Developmental Psychology, a Master's and Doctorate in Metaphysics and Transpersonal Counseling. Lisa has authored 7 books, speaks around the country, hosts Goddess workshops & retreats and is available for individual consultation. You can check out her website at http://doctorlisamsmith.com/.

www.ingramcontent.com/pod-product-compliance
Lightning Source LLC
LaVergne TN
LVHW011155080426
835508LV00007B/411